GW00870469

Dear Mel
Heres for your
future a conve
See
with lo
Ju

The Life Changing Magic of Setting Goals

Julie Hogbin

On Point Series
The life Changing Magic of Setting Goals – How to Set Goals for Inspiring and Sustaining Action.

ISBN-13: 978-153072974

Published by
10-10-10 Publishing
Markham, Ontario
Canada

Copyright © February 2016
by Julie Hogbin
London, England, United Kingdom

www.OnPointSeries.com
www.WealthWiseWomen.uk
www.BusinessTalksandWorkshops.com
www.SmartPropertyUK.com

All Rights Reserved

No part of this book may be reproduced in any form, by photocopying or by electronic or mechanical means, including information storage or retrieval systems, without permission in writing from both the copyright owner and the publisher of this book. This book is not intended to give any legal, medical, and/or financial advice to the readers.

For information about special discounts for bulk purchases, please contact 10-10-10 Publishing at 1-888-504-6257
Printed in the United States of America

Contents

Foreword

This book will seriously help you achieve whatever goal you want to achieve, regardless of who you are, and at whatever stage you are in Life or Business.

Julie has shared her knowledge of working with Entrepreneurs, Business and Individuals over 20 plus years, and has written this book to support you in achieving the results you desire.

We all need a plan, but we also need to be able to identify and remove that which stops us from executing the plan to a successful outcome. The author's ability to connect the dots and provide you with the solutions to the inner workings of your unconscious have never been put together in one book until now.

This book covers both the technical skills required to develop a strategy and to physically write the goals to make the plan live and, more importantly, it looks at the physiological aspects of how to achieve the planned goals.

It is easy to read and understand, and it will enable you to connect the dots yourself and achieve what you set out to do.

Raymond Aaron
NYTimes Bestselling Author

Dedication

With all my heart I dedicate this book to my parents, Joyce & Eric Hogbin. Without them I wouldn't be on the planet and, more importantly I would not have grown to be the person I am today.

Their love and support throughout my life, to each other and to me, is invaluable. They have set sound examples for me to follow and I am one very lucky daughter to have landed on their doorstep.

Mum and Dad, I love you with all my heart xx

and Dad I miss you so much 31.12.1922 - 17.08.2014

Acknowledgements

I have referenced my knowledge and learning from over 5 decades on the planet and my 30 plus years in the Learning & Personal Development world working with Individuals, Entrepreneurs & many, many Leadership Teams in Business as a Coach, Mentor, Trainer and Facilitator

I thank those that have provided me with the opportunities to 'practice' on them, those that have challenged me along the way and those that I study though observations on my travels – some of you will know who you are and the majority will never know.

I also thank the online and offline resources as mentioned along with quotes from some great individuals who changed the face of personal development with their work.
Forbes
Harvard Business Review
Simply Psychology & Psychology Studies
Google
Wikipedia

Albert Einstein, Abraham Maslow, David John Oates, Steven R Covey, Peter Drucker, Bob Proctor, Vilfredo Parato, to name just a few.

Changing the face of personal development changes the individuals that access their legacies, and I thank them from the bottom of my heart for the ideas they had, the research they initiated, and their fortitude to conclude it.

Plus I thank the 10-10-10 team for 'nagging' me with a purpose!

And my partner Stewart for looking after me, keeping me on track, providing inspiration and moral support plus keeping me fed and fuelled whilst in the midst of my writing xxxx

About Julie

Julie is 'just Julie' in her eyes; a normal person, with a normal upbringing, who went from being an almost straight A student to leaving the education system without a single qualification the first day she could. She has worked every day since either for others or more importantly for herself.

She does sometimes wonder how went from being a shy little girl hiding behind her Mum's skirts to now talking on stage and changing people's lives and businesses success. If you want to be inspired, talk to her!

Julie was awarded an Inspirational award by her colleagues in her last partnership. She always has a smile, she loves life and is willing and prepared to learn and change. Her intelligence and common sense has been utilised throughout her life, enabling her to change jobs and disciplines, challenge and inspire others and to generally do what she loves doing, whether that is working for herself or others.

She has taken the opportunities she either made happen or was offered, even when her heart was thumping!

She has said yes to opportunities when she had no idea how to do what was being offered, but doing so took her closer to her goal.

So is she normal? She thinks so, but other people tell her no.

The author currently lives in Kent, The Garden of England where she is a Leadership Consultant and Property Investor who runs networking events, seminars and on line programmes to support individuals and businesses develop their potential.

Julie has worked across both the Public and Private sector with individuals and teams, and more recently with start-ups and entrepreneurs.

With this book, she shares her years of experience and in-depth knowledge, that has helped many individuals and businesses achieve more with less, through the harnessing of human motivation, both theirs and their teams.

Currently Julie owns and operates multiple business streams in both Property and in the Personal and Business Development world.

www.OnPointSeries.com
www.WealthWiseWomen.uk
www.BusinessTalksandWorkshops.com
www.SmartPropertyUK.com

She helps businesses and aspiring entrepreneurs develop their interpersonal and business skills, and specifically wants to work with Women who, like her in the past, want to change their life.

One of her passions is to see run-down and underutilised properties come back to life, working in partnership with the owners, helping them to move comfortably into the next phase of their life with more money in their pocket, less worry in their head and in charge of their destination.

Factor 1 – The Context of Goal Setting

An Understanding of What It's All About

For decades, goal setting has been promoted as the panacea for improving individual, employee and organisational motivation for performance. Part of me agrees that it is; whether consciously or unconsciously we are goal driven creatures, and everything we do is goal driven!

So what does this mean? Whether we want to believe it or not, everything we do or don't do is within our control. Whether we are conscious or unconscious of what is driving us, something always is!

It is also true that 80% of people don't like consciously setting goals but are good with solving problems. There is a mind shift in how to view those things that we desire to achieve, and for some of us it is not a subtle mind shift, but a mind shift that has to be cracked with a sledgehammer.

Unless we are in total alignment with ourselves and our goals, we will be constantly in conflict, internally and potentially externally, about what to do, how to do it and when to do it.

This is called relational dialectics, which basically means we are in relationship with ourselves and others, and that to do one thing may cause tension with another thing.

Let me provide you with some very basic examples:

* You love spending time on your own and you want to be in a relationship.
* You would prefer not to talk about yourself and you want to build your business.
* You want to become fitter and you dislike exercise.
* You want to be a size smaller and you love chocolate.
* You want to apply for a new job and you dislike interviews.
* You enjoy the feel of a book in your hand and you know an electronic reader is lighter to carry.

Our lives are full of these dialectics, and once we acknowledge they exist we can choose to do something about them.

We are all goal driven at every point of our day, and as much as some of the following activities may not be seen as positive, they are all achieving a goal that we have.

* Slumped in a chair watching a soap, a documentary or reality TV
* Attending three networking events a week to capture 45 new contacts
* Sitting staring into space for an hour
* Building a business worth 1, 2 or 50 million pounds
* Taking your parents to lunch
* Being on Google when you know a deadline is looming
* Aimlessly (apparently) reviewing the jobs vacant ads
* Drinking a bottle of wine to ourselves

Everything we do is goal driven. Some we are aware of and others we aren't!

A piece of research indicated that only 3% of the population have acknowledged goals and only 1% of those have goals written down.

Research has proven that those with Goals written down achieve far, far, far more than those that don't!

So what happens to the other 97% and in which % do you sit?

The bad news, and I personally wish it to be different, is that it is not quite that simple. The skill of creating goals and orchestrating the process of achieving them is an art form and a skill.

The good news is that we can all do it. It is a skill that can be learnt, practiced and mastered.

Across hundreds of experiments and thousands of participants across four continents, the results are clear:

'Specific, challenging goals boost performance'

Locke, Latham, Smith, & Wood 1990

But there is a big BUT.

So long as the person is committed to the goal, has the necessary ability to achieve it, and does not have conflicting goals, there is a positive, direct relationship between goal difficulty and task performance.

Rather than being an 'over-the-counter' remedy for boosting performance, goal setting should be thought through, monitored, reviewed, evaluated and adjusted when required.

Lessons from the Aviation world

> **A plane is off course up to 95% of the time!**
> **Through automated flight systems they are adjusted back on track and arrive at their prescribed destination within a few minutes of their original arrival time.**

It might be a good idea for us human beings to take a page from the airlines with regards to our own lives and chosen paths. Is it so hard to admit that perhaps we might be in need of some sort of correction?

* Why do we cling so tightly to our way of being?
* Why won't we change our path, even when we see a disaster looming on the horizon?
* Are we scanning the skies, so to speak, for the next change or the next collision?

We start our lives full of joy, without fear, open and ready to try anything and everything, and along the way 'something' happens to us! Think about yourself as a child; you would never have learned how to walk, run, skip if every time you fell over you made the decision that you would fail the next time you tried.

Goal setting is a powerful process for thinking about your ideal future, and for motivating yourself to turn your vision of this future into reality. Achievers in all fields and disciplines set goals, and it is not just setting them and creating a written plan that makes them successful – achievers actually work the plan!

The plan becomes a living entity, not just completed once a year because it 'has' to be! It becomes habit, and is rarely if ever written as a 'new year's resolution.'

The plan becomes dog-eared; it is visited, reviewed, used, adjusted to suit and has a life of its own to keep you on track.

What is achievable?

Goals will support you to achieve your desire in all walks of life:

* Creating Wealth – through whichever means you choose
* Building & Creating Business
* Becoming an Author
* Building, Creating & Sustaining Relationships
* Health
* Developing your Career
* Life
* Hobbies
* Holidays
* Change
* Finding the partner of your dreams

In fact, setting goals will increase our chance of success in every walk of our life

Setting goals supports you to:

* Choose where you want to go in life
* Know where to concentrate your efforts
* Know when you are off track
* Know when you are on track
* Be clear in your communication
* Focus
* Refuse requests from others

* Accept requests from others
* Look for opportunities
* Know who to speak to
* Create your 'elevator' pitch
* Celebrate success when you achieve your goal
* Acquire knowledge
* Practically apply theory into practice
* Manage your time
* Manage your resources
* etc etc etc

Focus and Energy

Without a goal where are you directing your energies? What path are you travelling? What distractions are getting in the way? What normal everyday habits are stopping you?

Where your Focus goes your Energy flows

If you don't take the time to focus on what matters to you, what is important to you, what you want and need.

Then you will either live the life of someone else's design, or the life that you design unconsciously or think is the life you 'should' live.

Research has found that if you have specific goals you are more likely to have higher performance. Specific in this instance means with a specific deadline and purpose, with a time, a day, a year.

Goals that stretch you will lead to growth and higher performance – if we feel they are too easy we are not motivated by them and if we feel they are out of our reach we will not even attempt them.

When you really commit to and accept the goals, you are more likely to attain higher performance. Commitment is one of the main psychological influencers in society, so if we cannot commit to ourselves how successful will we be with our commitment to others?

What does commitment really mean?

Research over the years indicates that commitment lies deep within us, and our commitment will direct our actions with a quiet power to be and to appear consistent with what we have already done.

We convince ourselves that we have made the right choice, and that we feel better about the decisions we make.

Therefore when we choose to do something differently than we have done before we are challenging our unconscious to change our previous habits and our previous commitments to ourself.

Martin Luther King

Martin Luther King made fabulous speeches about his Dream, and he was very clear in what he wanted his legacy to be. To this day that legacy lives on. His passion fired change and motivated a nation.

An excerpt of one of the speeches is detailed, which clearly identifies he knew there would be trials and tribulations, that it would not be easy or smooth, and that faith and action would be required in huge quantities.

An excerpt from Martin Luther King Jr speech from August 1963

"And so even though we face the difficulties of today and tomorrow, I still have a dream. It is a dream deeply rooted in the American dream.

I have a dream that one day this nation will rise up and live out the true meaning of its creed: "We hold these truths to be self-evident, that all men are created equal."

I have a dream that one day on the red hills of Georgia, the sons of former slaves and the sons of former slave owners will be able to sit down together at the table of brotherhood.

I have a dream that one day even the state of Mississippi, a state sweltering with the heat of injustice, sweltering with the heat of oppression, will be transformed into an oasis of freedom and justice.

I have a dream that my four little children will one day live in a nation where they will not be judged by the colour of their skin but by the content of their character.

I have a dream today!

I have a dream that one day, down in Alabama, with its vicious racists, with its governor having his lips dripping with the words of "interposition" and "nullification" -- one day right there in Alabama little black boys and black girls will be able to join hands with little white boys and white girls as sisters and brothers.

I have a dream today!

I have a dream that one day every valley shall be exalted, and every hill and mountain shall be made low, the rough places will be made plain, and the crooked places will be made straight; "and the glory of the Lord shall be revealed and all flesh shall see it together."

This is our hope, and this is the faith that I go back to the South with. With this faith, we will be able to hew out of the mountain of despair a stone of hope. With this faith, we will be able to transform the jangling discords of our nation into a beautiful symphony of brotherhood. With this faith, we will be able to work together, to pray together, to struggle together, to go to jail together, to stand up for freedom together, knowing that we will be free one day."

The legacy that was spoken about in this speech was a huge, and what may have appeared impossible, goal at the time. But with the passion with which the goal was expressed, the world changed. Many, many lessons can be learnt from history, and if we choose to we can apply them to our lives. This speech clearly shows that belief and passion can ignite others, but belief and passion alone are not enough. We need a plan and action, along with many other characteristics

Feedback and Accountability

Feedback and accountability on performance against the goal will lead to higher performance. You can, of course, hold yourself to account and provide yourself with feedback. But it is without a doubt far more effective when the feedback is received from a third party, and you are held to account by that third party.

Accountability and feedback are far more respected by yourself when received from somebody you respect. If you do not respect them, there will be a tendency to reject the feedback and take no notice of any attempt to be held to account.

In your personal life you have an absolute choice of your accountability partner. When you are working within a business as an employee generally the person holding you to account and providing you with feedback will be your boss!

When there is a deadline attached to the goal it proves to be motivational. Let me ask you a question – do you work with more focus closer to a deadline looming?

Who can you access to keep you accountable?

Whether you have small or large dreams, setting goals allows you to plan how you want to move through life. Some achievements can take a lifetime to attain, while others can be completed in the course of a day. Whether you're setting totally audacious goals, broad overarching aims or planning specific manageable goals, you will feel a sense of accomplishment and self-worth, and your confidence will grow as you succeed.

Factor 2 - Your Dream and Your Legacy

***Are you living a life in regret or joy?**

What are your unfulfilled ambitions?*

The basic thought process

You need to be real and honest with yourself and dig deep to really and truly establish what you want to do.

Imagine that you are at the end of your life.

- What do you have?
- What have you achieved?
- What philanthropic activities have you completed?
- What group of people have you worked with?
- What business have you built?
- What level have you achieved with your career?
- What qualifications do you have?
- What countries have you travelled?
- What family do you have?

This list is not designed to be overwhelming; it is a list designed to provide you with a thought process and vision to plan towards achieving.

This is the point where everything that you have ever wanted to be and do is put on the table for you to work through and make life decisions.

A few questions for you to think through:

- If you died today are you at the place where you want to be?
- What is on your bucket list?
- What is the legacy you wanted to create?
- Have you even thought about the legacy you want to leave?
- What 'things' do you want to complete?
- When will you start the 'things' that are on your life to do list?
- What is on your life to do list?
- What business do you want to start?
- Are you in the relationship of your dreams with yourself or others?

Somebody mentioned to me recently that Goal setting is alright but it really doesn't allow for those really big 'hairy arsed' goals that some people have.

How wrong can they be? That is exactly what goal setting allows you to achieve!

Somebody mentioned to me recently that Goal setting is alright but it really doesn't allow for those really big 'hairy arsed' goals that some people have.

How wrong can they be?
That is exactly what goal setting allows you to achieve!

*** Do you spring out of bed in the morning with a smile on your face and passion for the day? ***

Where are you now?

It can sometimes be the most difficult part to acknowledge and recognise where you are, as this is the reality of the life you have created for yourself.

Where are you now? Are you at someone else's beck and call with no time for yourself? Look back at the previous chapter and identify your reality compared to the lists identified.

The need for honesty with self-awareness is crucial at this point

One day I said over and over again One day I will be free One day I will be happy One day I will be wealthy One day I will be healthy One day I said over and over again One day...................... I dream of change I dream of success One day.................... I dream not one day I dream this day	I create this day in every moment I choose success I choose change I choose happiness I choose to think I choose to focus My path diverges and which one do I follow as I cannot travel both My choice the one less known My choice the one less worn My choice the one to my dream Julie Hogbin 2015

What has led you to where you are now? Self-awareness is key to change. You need to recognise where you are and how you got there.

What choices have you made in life to get you to here? Every day in every moment, the choices you make create your life.

Every action has a consequence and result, and every repeated action has a greater result.

The Wheel of Life – are your spokes broken?

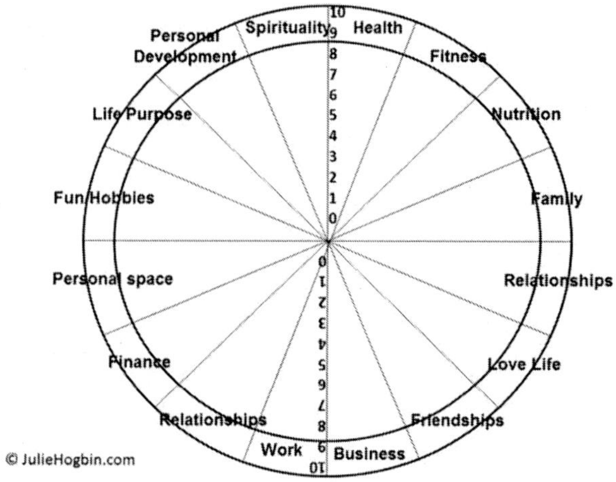

The sectioned circle is called the *'Wheel of Life.'* It is a model used in Coaching and the personal development field.

It will help you decide what areas of your life it would be beneficial to work on and which you need to give priority to.

The aim is to achieve more balance in all the important areas of your life.

Rate your level of satisfaction in each area of your life. Zero indicates you are not satisfied and 10 means highly satisfied.

This particular wheel (and there are many) suggests some, but not all, of the areas you may want to consider. You can make it as detailed as you want, and change the words to suit your life and vocabulary. I have thought of 3 more you may want to consider: career, pension, and investments. The earlier you do this, the greater the result will be long-term.

Personalise the wheel to your situation, your life, your career, your business.

After rating yourself, connect the sections so you will have a full picture. The wheel will very probably have uneven spokes. The objective is to improve the areas of your life so they are balanced and working in harmony.

When your life is in harmony and the wheel has even spokes, the journey you choose to travel will be smoother. Imagine driving a car or riding a bike with one flat tyre. The car is less manoeuvrable, less responsive, takes more energy and effort to drive, and ultimately it takes you longer to get to your destination. This is exactly the same as the wheel of life; if one critical spoke is very low it will affect all of the others.

You will probably find that in some areas you score highly and in others lower – this is the first stage to looking at what you may want or need to work on. You will be able to identify the areas that will become your priority.

***Flip forward to Factor 8 and read Pareto Principle section to support you in identifying your priority area**

Be honest with yourself and stay focused on the positive outcome it is the start of your plan for moving forward in whatever direction you choose.

Dare to Dream – Dream Big and Sparkly

This is your opportunity to really think about what you want. What dreams do you have that are unfulfilled in your current circumstances? You may have identified them through your Wheel of Life or they may not have appeared there.

Dare to dream, and remember how to. If the joy of dreaming has deserted you, relearn the skill. As a child you would have dreamed and played in a world of make-believe that for you was real. There is no reason why as adults we cannot re-access that world to create a future with a plan.

> **You are never too old to set another goal or to dream a new dream.**
>
> **C. S. Lewis**

> **You have to dream before your dreams can come true.**
>
> **A. P. J. Abdul Kalam**

If you're not clear where you want to be you will end up somewhere else. The choices are many, as are the distractions along the way. There is a phenomenon called the 'shiny penny' syndrome, which basically means without a plan, without focus, you will see something that appears attractive, interesting and exciting and that will divert you for a short or long-term period of time, away from where you really want to go.

It is a little like walking through a maze; there may be many dead ends, it may be frustrating, you may feel like giving up and when you are truly 'in it' giving up is not an option as the only way out is through the centre.

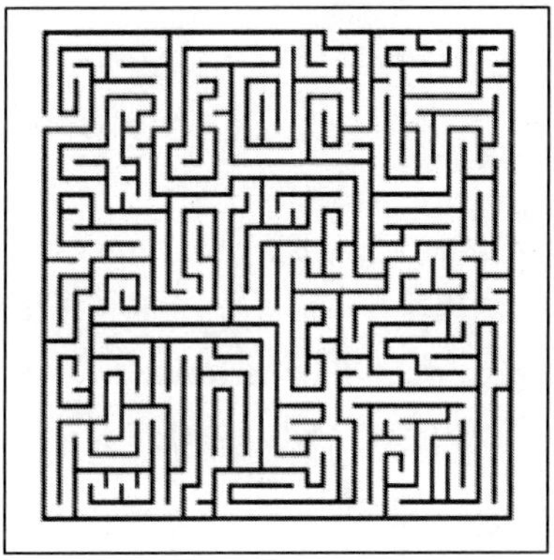

The trick is to clearly identify where you want to be in the future – dream big because this will be your inspiration and your foundation to work from.

Apart from the general areas that have already been identified, think outside of the norm

- What were your dreams as a child?
- What did you always want to be?
- What have you always wanted to do?

- What's your secret desire that you have never told anyone and kept a secret?
- Where or who do you want to visit before it or they disappear?

True story

In 2011 when I was first told to write a book by my then mentor, not only was I terrified at the thought, my response was what have I got to write about? Me? I can't write; I left school without any exams! (go figure)

With over 5 decades of life and 30+ years of business I now think I have a lot to write about, I am very happy to say, this is the 1st of a few books in my head.

The only thing that got in the way was my very own personal limiting beliefs - yes in the plural. We all have them and sometimes it takes someone else to recognise them, challenge them and unleash our true potential. This really is where feedback and an accountability partner, come in very handy.

What do I mean by limiting belief? It is that state of mind where you think something is the truth without there being any real evidence of the fact. If it is a limiting belief it will stop you from doing the thing that you want to do without you really understanding why, unless you choose to stop and question the thought processes that you are having.

- You believe you can't so you don't.
- You believe you are unable so you are.
- You believe you are non-deserving so you stop even before you start.

There are, of course, empowering beliefs, which are the ones that allow you to move mountains where others can only move a molehill.

- You believe you can so you do.
- You believe you are able so you are.
- You believe you deserve so you achieve.

Who else will be affected?

You are thinking about changing your life and setting goals so you can create and live your dream. Whilst you are creating this dream it is good to think about who else will be affected.

Think about your family, your children, your partner, your parents, your friends and loved ones. Think about your work environment and your home environment.

Think about who you associate with now and who you may associate with when you change your life. Your habits may change; in fact they probably will, and this will potentially affect your relationships.

When you change your life, unless you are a complete loner it will have an impact on those around you.

Your new you may want to associate with those that have different habits. It may be a positive mind-set versus the negative mind-set that you may be choosing to leave.

They may drink less, eat less, exercise more, have more intelligent conversations; they may have more money than your normal circle of friends – the list is almost endless. By changing your habits you will become a different person to your normally associated network.

This leads into how you communicate your change, whatever that may be, and the affect that may have on others. Some people you may choose to leave behind, some people you may want to take with you, and some people may not want to come with you. This can include your family and your best friends.

Be prepared; it happens.

A true personal story:

In 2011 I decided to leave my job as a partner in a consultancy, change my career, go on a trip of personal discovery and really find out what I truly wanted to do with the rest of my life. This included, attending multi speaker events, walking on fire, trading FOREX, creating websites, dabbling with MLM and finally resting with property investing (there is a lot more to the story of course).

At that time I had two 'best' friends. One I had known for over 20 years; we went out together, we socialised together, we went on holiday together. I had been there for her through the birth of her daughter, her husband's illness, and later their divorce and a few other events. I was once told that when she was feeling down she would phone me for a chat to lift her spirits. She once described me as the positive bouncing ball that she followed and tried to catch. A good friend, or so I thought.

We talked about everything, and please read that in the past tense. We did talk about everything until I started to talk about things that were different, things that weren't the norm, and people that were outside of our current network. At that point I started to see a glazed look come over her eyes and her head turn away. I could see that this made it very uncomfortable for my other friend. That was one thing – but what was I supposed to talk about? My new life was exciting, I was learning new things, I was experimenting, I was meeting new people & I wanted to share it with my best friend.

It got to a point where I said very little when we went out, other than to ask questions as to how her life was and to sit and listen to the answer all evening. It was, to be honest, tiring and a one way street, which is not what a true friendship is about. So I broached a conversation between us to see what could be done.

I was told: "I don't understand it." so I offered to explain 'it' if she wanted to understand more, than I had already shared. I was then told "I don't understand it and I don't agree with it." a little bit of a kick in the teeth, you could say, and a bizarre statement which was repeated a few times.

In my world - How can you possibly not agree with something you do not understand? The conversation went around the houses a little at that point as I attempted to understand the thought processes. In reality, even today, I don't. Maybe she didn't like me changing and just wasn't able to communicate it. Maybe it scared her. Who knows?

I made a decision with the facts I had at hand that our 'friendship' was to end.

It may seem harsh on paper, but it took 15 months to get to that point, when the negativity that surrounded me when we met was not sustainable for me.

What would you have done? My other best friend is still my best friend and has a completely different approach and understanding of what my life has *become. It doesn't mean that she fully agrees with everything I do and have done, but at least she is willing to accept the different me (even though I am fundamentally still the same me).*

And of course this is only my side of the story and I did what I could to find out the other side of the story.

Your new goal setting habits for your success may take you into unchartered waters; well, definitely waters that your colleagues, friends, family and loved ones are not used to.

Communication of your changes is important to get them on your side and working with you. I have more stories to tell about others I have 'lost' and kept along the way.

The highest form of ignorance is when you reject something you don't know anything about - Dr Wayne Dyer

What else will be affected?

A lot is the easy answer - this is a key point that very often gets overlooked or forgotten. The changes may be short or long-term and, when managed, result in your success.

Let me explain what I mean.

There will always be consequences to any change of behaviour, which is exactly what you will be doing if you are looking to achieve a different result than what you have now.

For every action there is a reaction-it is a simple 3rd natural law of physics as identified by Sir Isaac Newton

For everything you do there is an equal and opposite reaction. When you push you will probably get pushed back; if you pull people will come with you.

Referencing back to relational dialectics, you are also in relation with yourself so if you push yourself you are more than likely to push yourself back, and resist the change you want.

If you pull yourself into the new 'thing' you will more likely come with you!

We can achieve nothing without paying the price, and our results are directly proportional to our investment. That means time, energy, effort, and on occasion money.

As an example, what if you are looking to change your diet? You may currently, on your route around the supermarkets, go down the sweet aisle. To change your eating habits, you will need to change movement around the supermarket to reduce temptation, and this will need to be a conscious decision to stop you. You may have to move your trolley to the fruit and veg department for a while!

If you have a partner or children at home who likes sweets, what will the impact be on them and then on the temptation for you?

It may be you are looking to develop information around a new subject, which will take time from your normal activities. You may be at home reading books, watching DVDS, films, documentaries, or listening to audio on your travels.

Which may mean:

- That you won't be watching the soaps, which will change what you are to talk about
- You won't be going out with your friends or family
- You won't be reading the newspaper on your journey to work
- You won't be listening to your favourite music on your travels

Not all the changes are negative. If you are looking to change your job to earn more money, your holidays may improve or get better, you may be able to buy that new car you've always wanted or to buy a new house that you've seen. On the other side of that, you will have to develop new relationships with new work colleagues and say goodbye to the old ones.

If you are reading this book while working within business, it may be that you want to improve your Leadership skills and to improve your credibility within the working environment. One of the things you may need to change is the information that you chat about around the water cooler or the coffee machine.

The information you share can never be taken back. It may be that you change socialising habits with those you work with. Leadership and Management can be a lonely place, but can also be an extraordinarily rewarding place. Boundaries set very early on are key to long-term success in your Leadership role and career development.

With all these changes there will be pros and cons – pre-warned is pre-armed as the saying goes, so think about this in advance and you will be able to manage the changes more effectively; both your habits and other people's expectations and reactions when they appear – as they will.

A true personal story:

I had a good life by a lot of people's standards. I was earning decent money, went on at least two holidays a year, I had taken an additional months unpaid holiday, a year to spend more time with my parents, and I bought a new car every 3 or 4 years. I worked really hard -- 70 hours a week or more. I still had a years' worth of targets, even though I had taken a pay cut and only worked 11 months. I travelled from one end of the country to the other to carry out my duties, staying away from home overnight on many occasions, and not always in nice places.

Now I work from home, mostly, and can work any hours of the day or night. I spent two years taking Mum & Dad out and spending quality time with them. I spent from May 2014 to August 2014 with Mum at hospital visiting Dad, and I can now visit Mum whenever I want to. My parents were and are very important to me.

I now see my house as a liability rather than an asset as it costs me money – so until I fully achieve my plan I have two carefully chosen lodgers as well. I haven't bought a new car and I haven't been on holiday apart from working breaks, and only twice in three years. I have been on business trips and attended seminars.

The pros of my new lifestyle far outweigh the cons – it's not always easy but it's all possible, and every day I get closer to my dream, my way, my choice, in my own time and all with a very carefully crafted plan.

Live a few years of your life like most people won't, so that you can spend the rest of your life like most people can't.

STOP – What is your WHY?

Before you read any further – I am going to ask you to think about your WHY – why are you doing this 'thing'? Or even thinking about doing this 'thing'? Whatever it may be.

Your why is your driving force, it is your cause, it is your force for good and it will be personal to you. You may be doing it for someone else BUT -- and it's a big BUT -- it's because you WANT to, not because you have been told to.

You may have been told to get fitter for a medical reason BUT if you are not doing it for YOU it will be so, so much harder. More about this as you read through the book.

A true story:

When I started my journey, my why at the time, was about earning a fortune, going on umpteen holidays a year, having a mortgage free house with enough money in the bank to do what I want, when I want, with who I want – with hindsight I wasn't thinking clearly, it was all materialistic and I had got caught up in the hype of high emotion upsells and the dreams that people 'put' in my head!

When I gathered my thoughts and really thought about why I was doing what I did it was:
Spending quality time with my parents - this is absolutely key for me.

Setting an example to others, that they too can take charge of their life and their pension effectively, rather than relying on the government.
And all the rest of the material items came much further down the line.

My plan was adjusted to suit my true why and because time is finite I have taken longer to get to where I am aiming for out of choice, I still take actions every day to get me to where I want to be, and where I want to stay. I am on track and focused, and get to spend quality time with Mum.

Take time to really think about your Why - why are you proposing to do what you are thinking about? Remember who you are and what you do, and remind yourself of your core values. If you attempt something that goes against your basic principles you will fight every step of the way to achieve it and you may never get there – which can become soul destroying.

Conflict – it will occur; welcome it

The change may put you into a conflict scenario, which may be an internal conflict with yourself or external with others.

A definition of conflict I work with in WealthWiseWomen.uk and BusinessTalksandWorkshops.com is:

'Conflict is a struggle between at least two interdependent parties who perceive incompatible goals, scarce rewards and interference from the other party in achieving their goals'

Hocker & Wilmot

Read the definition through and analyse it for yourself; truly understand the words and the meaning of them.

This definition is powerful in reminding us that parties within a conflict have some level of interdependence – if they did not, they would not be in conflict in the first place.

It also reminds us that conflict comes about because of perceptions, not necessarily because of facts. It is in the understanding and respecting of each other's perceptions that most conflict resolution lies.

Communicate the meaning behind your goal to others that will be affected by it and gain their buy in to your cause.

Reward yourself and others during and after the success. Interference can sometime appear to be so because someone is attempting to help! Now that is an interesting thought process to get your head round.

Types of Conflict

1	Intrapersonal	Within self
2	Interpersonal	Between individuals
3	Intragroup	Within a group
4	Intergroup	Between groups
5	International	Between nations

It is recognised that there are various types of conflicts. With change you will definitely be affecting level 1. Depending on the change what other levels are you affecting? What legacy are you looking to leave, and will that take you to dealing with level 5?

There is an immutable conflict at work in life and in business, a constant battle between peace and chaos. Neither can be mastered, but both can be influenced. How you go about that is the key to success.

Phil Knight

Factor 3 – Mission and Vision

Interestingly enough, whatever you read, whatever definitions you look at, whichever book you pick up around building, developing and creating a life we all want as individuals or businesses – it will mention mission and vision, and further along the line a plan.

That is the commonality and then everyone attempts to explain mission and vision, clarify them and talk about how to create them. I have a far simpler view. You need all three of them, and when thinking about 'mission and vision' which one comes first is unimportant. If they are created together and then separated so be it – if they get slightly intermingled at the beginning it's not important, just as long as they are done.

Without mission and vision you wander without purpose or cause.

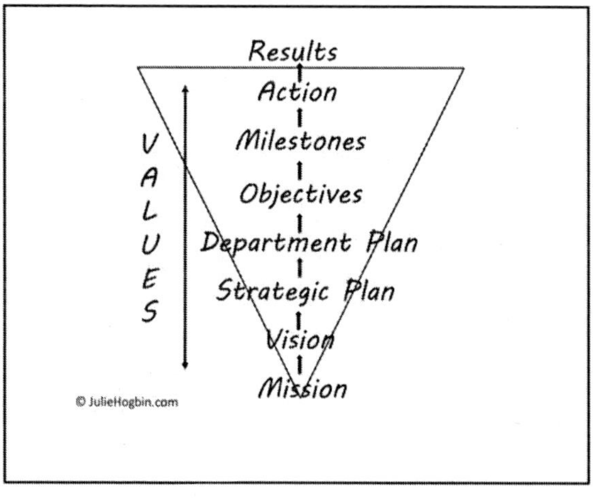

They are the foundation of any strategic planning and goal setting.

Without them, don't be surprised if the results you get are not what you wanted!

The further up the model you travel, the more detailed your plan becomes, and your values remain in focus and in alignment.

So now on to attempting to clarify what they are – people use the words interchangeably, as it all depends on how they were taught and who taught them. As long as you know what you mean and can express it well, your job is done.

A mission is different from a vision in that:

- Mission is the cause, the what and the who, why it exists
- Vision is the effect, the why and the how, and needs to be inspirational

A mission is something to be accomplished whereas a vision is something to be pursued for that accomplishment. You may want to share both when gaining buy-in from others

Creating your Mission Statement

A mission statement is a statement of the purpose of an organisation or an individual. It is the organisation or individual's reason for existing and is a written declaration of the core purpose and focus.

It is like a goal for what the company wants to do for the world; it has been described as your earthly destiny, and will be short and concise.

It normally remains unchanged over time, but even that isn't set in stone as organisations and individuals recreate themselves to survive.

Some non-profit Mission examples:

TED: Spreading Ideas. (2)

Smithsonian: The increase and diffusion of knowledge. (6)

CARE: To serve individuals and families in the poorest communities in the world. (12)

The Nature Conservancy: To conserve the lands and waters on which all life depends. (11)

Make-A-Wish: We grant the wishes of children with life-threatening medical conditions to enrich the human experience with hope, strength and joy. (21)

Some for profit mission examples:

Agco: Profitable growth through superior customer service, innovation, quality and commitment.(10)

Disney: We create happiness by providing the finest in entertainment for people of all ages, everywhere.(15)

Nike: to lead in corporate citizenship through proactive programs that reflect caring for the world family of Nike, our teammates, our consumers, and those who provide services to Nike. To bring inspiration and innovation to every athlete* in the world. *If you have a body, you are an athlete. (48)

Virgin Atlantic: To grow a profitable airline, where people love to fly and people love to work (15)

In business and for individuals, changes are made to unlock new dimensions of revenue and profitability, heights that would never have been reached by staying on the original course. The one constant in business and life is change; organisations change the service they provide to survive.

Organisations and individuals need to be fleet of foot and access foresight to recognise that existing strategies are ill-suited to the future marketplace. This allows change to occur and enables fundamental shifts in focus.

An example of this in the current economic climate is the increase of businesses trading online and supplying their goods through Amazon or eBay. With fulfilment and drop shipping, the need for actually carrying stock and storing stock is now no longer existent.

This has opened up an opportunity for anyone to open up their own retail outlet online, without the huge setup costs that a high street shop requires.

Just one example of how organisations change their service to meet a changing environment and economic need.

Nokia was originally founded in 1865 as a ground wood pulp mill, in 1898 it moved from wood pulping to become a Rubber mill, in 1900 it became involved with Electricity generation, in the 1970s Telecommunications were Nokia's 'thing' and in 2013 they sold the mobile phone arm to Microsoft! In 2014 Nokia started to work with China Mobile.

It's a long journey from a Wood Pulp Mill to Telecommunications and from 1865 to 2014 as an organisation they have remained in business, although different service, for 150 years.

Properly crafted mission statements:

- Create focus to keep you on track
- Act as a filter to identify what is important from what is not
- Identify your target market
- State the service and product that will be provided
- Indicate the geographical area you will operate within
- Provide a framework and guide for strategic decision making
- Communicate a sense of intended direction to the entire organisation
- Distinguish you from the rest of the market.

A mission statement will cover all or some of the above.

A personal mission statement is developed in much the same way that an organisational mission statement is created, and may also change over time.

A personal mission statement is a brief description of what an individual wants to focus on, accomplish and become. It is a way to focus energy, actions, behaviours and decisions towards the things that are most important to the individual.

Creating the Vision

> **Vision without action is daydreaming and action without vision is a nightmare.**
>
> **Chinese Proverb**

***Your buy-in to your vision is key to your motivation for success and happiness.**

Julie Hogbin*

Setting lifetime visionary goals gives you the overall perspective that shapes all other aspects of your decision-making.

The thought process will also allow you to communicate to others with clarity and confidence, and gain their buy-in to your vision.

Make sure that the goals you have set are ones that you genuinely want to achieve, whether you are working alone or with others.

The practice of goal-setting is not just helpful. Psychologists tell us that people who make consistent progress toward meaningful goals live happier more satisfied lives than those who do not

We need first to lead ourselves before we can lead anybody else and in the words of Warren Bennis "Leadership is the capacity to translate vision into reality."

So what is a vision? A vision is the art of seeing what is invisible to others; it is the process of developing the biggest picture you can in all its glory

Thoughts become things. If you see it in your mind, you will hold it in your hand.

Bob Proctor

Be daring, be different, be impractical, be anything that will assert integrity of purpose and imaginative vision against the play-it-safers, the creatures of the commonplace, the slaves of the ordinary.

Cecil Beaton

A vision needs to be inspiring to you, and if working with others to them as well. Organisations spend 10s of 1,000s of pounds, dollars, euros on creating refining and communicating their vision.

A true story:

In one area of my business the mission I have adopted is:

'No Bull, No Hype, just good old-fashioned solid information. Teaching property investors how to properly and legally at value driven prices.' And that is how I market it big and bold.

I adopted that because it is true and it is my philosophy in life. I am honest, direct and transparent, and I want the world to know. BUT the industry that his particular business operates within is known for its 'shark-infested' waters, so I make my promise very clear to my customers.

Virgin Rail Vision - We want to use our passion for innovation and customer service to deliver attractive rail services in more countries.

10 words

Harvard Vision - Harvard College will set the standard for residential liberal arts and sciences education in the twenty-first century. We are committed to creating and sustaining the conditions that enable all Harvard College students to experience an unparalleled educational journey that is intellectually, socially, and personally transformative.

48 words

Your personal vision statement is the light shining in the darkness toward which you turn to find your way. It provides you with the philosophies and principles that guide your every decision and action.

Always Dream Big

SPARKLE like Crazy

Living with intention.

We can drive, direct and change our lives. All that's required is a shift in mind set and commitment to action.

What is your mission and vision? What is your earthly destiny? Think about it now and write it down. Think again, dig deeper, sleep on it, review it until it is solid for you.

Capture your first thought now - write it in pencil you can enhance it later

"Cherish your visions and your dreams as they are the children of your soul, the blueprints of your ultimate accomplishments."

Napoleon Hill

The Law of Attraction

The law of attraction states that every positive or negative event that happened to you was attracted by you.

This belief is based upon the idea that people and their thoughts are both made from "pure energy," and the belief that like energy attracts like energy.

There are no scientific studies that prove the theory to be true, but I have experienced too many coincidences to not believe it, which is why there is this short chapter in this book – if you are interested further there is plenty of information online, and the concept attracts a very large following.

A key to this is the true belief that it will work, and maintaining that belief whilst putting the thought into the Universe. For some of you I know this will be taking it one step too far; please remember to keep it in mind for future reference. The Law of Attraction also fits in to your vision board.

***See it, say it, write it, truly believe it both internally and externally, take action, persevere and it shall be yours**
Julie Hogbin*

True stories

My father was ill in 2014 and in hospital for a number of months and on an almost daily basis I used to take my mother in to visit. Parking at this particular inner city hospital is extremely difficult (to say the least) even with blue badge parking permissions.

When I put my mind to it, which was most days on the drive to the hospital, I either parked directly outside the hospital or within 100 yards. Other people who visited regularly walked over a mile after parking, and everybody in the hospital used to complain about the parking – I never had an issue not once

I receive phone calls from people I need to talk to whose numbers I do not have and I have not met previously.

I meet people I wanted to meet, at events in a crowd of thousands.

There is far too much evidence for me to disbelieve the concept.

We are using the law of attraction every second of every day. So if you are receiving what you want you are doing well. If you are receiving things that you are finding challenging start changing your thoughts. You have been attracted to reading this book – my question is what made you pick it up and buy it?

There are really only three basic steps: ask, believe, and receive. But of course there is a lot more to it than that.

Be sure about what you want, and when you do decide believe yourself without doubt. Remember that you're sending a request to the universe which is created by thoughts, and therefore responds to thoughts.

Know exactly what it is that you want. If you're unclear, the universe will get an unclear frequency and will send you unwanted results. So be sure it is something you have strong enthusiasm for.

Ask the Universe for it. Make your request. Send a picture of what you want to the universe; tell the universe, and others, what it is you want. The universe will answer. See this thing as already yours. The more detailed your vision, the better, which goes right back to the core of goal setting and getting your message out there.

Now the universe is a very kind and value-driven thing, so be prepared to give without expecting anything in return – reciprocity is another tool of influencing, and the universe believes in the laws as well.

Philosophy, Principle and Trust

The ancient Greek word philosophia was probably coined by Pythagoras and literally means 'love of wisdom' or 'friend of wisdom.' Philosophy is often distinguished from other ways of addressing problems by its questioning critical approach and its reliance on rational argument, and can refer to any body of knowledge. In everyday speak the term can refer to any of the most basic beliefs, concepts and attitudes of an individual or group.

A principle is a law that has to be and is followed. Principle can be defined as a universally applicable directing guideline. When you adopt a principled way of operating within it means that you adhere to your recognised set of belief systems. This provides you with increased clarity and focus.

So why do I mention philosophy, principle and trust in a book around setting goals and achieving success?

When you establish your philosophy and principals linked to your overarching mission it will allow you to base every decision you make from good solid fact supported with your belief structure

- It will lead you to feel confident and trust your decisions
- It will allow you to have confident communication with others
- It will provide you with a 'sounding board' to assess and evaluate against
- It will lead you to, in the face of change, create a way forward
- When you trust you, it will shine out, others will see it as true and trust you as well

It creates within you predictability and reliability; you become consistent in your actions and your message which then allows others to trust you, and you to trust yourself.

That trust can be with bodies external to you and also internal to you! Your unconscious plays a big part in whether you achieve your goals or not, more about this later in the book.

Trust comes from two areas in life. One is around us, who we are and how we choose to operate within the world, and the second is the assessment by others of how we operate.

Robert F Hurley from Fordham University in New York developed a model that can be used to predict whether an individual will trust or distrust in a given situation. The model identifies 10 factors that are considered in the decision-making process. The first three factors concern you, the decision-maker, the trustor. The other seven factors relate to aspects of a particular situation and the relationship between the trustor and the trustee.

Your unconscious needs to trust you when you are asking it to do something differently, otherwise it will not accept the request!

The first three factors enable us to make the decision and the questions to ask here are:

1. How risk tolerant is the trustor?
2. How well-adjusted to the world is the trustor?
3. How much power to sanction does the trustor have?

When asking these questions about yourself, the higher your risk tolerance is, the more likely you are to trust and the more likely you are to want to do something different.

The more well-adjusted you are to the world, seeing it as a benign place, full of benevolence and there to help and support you rather than hinder and interfere and do you bad, the more likely you are to trust others and do something different.

The greater the power you have and the ability to sanction or hold others to account, the more likely you are to make decisions and do something different.

If you answered each question on a scale of 1 to 10, one being low and 10 being high, the closer you are to 30 the more likely you are to trust both yourself and others to do the right thing and make the right decision.

The situational factors form seven questions – this is where you are working with others.

1. How secure do the parties feel? Some risks are greater than others.
2. How many similarities to the parties have in common? The more similarities the greater buy-in.
3. How well aligned are the parties? The more philosophies and principles that are held in common the better.
4. How much benevolent concern is displayed? If you would throw yourself in front of a flying bullet for them what they do the same for you?

5. How capable are they? Competence and ability play a big part in trust.
6. Have they indicated they are predictable and have integrity? They do what they say they will, when they say they will, with honesty.
7. What is the level of communication? The greater the communication the better the trust.

When you operate with trust and through your philosophies and principles, they will guide your every action and reaction. Identifying your principles first then allows you to communicate and behave through them.

Values in Life

When composing your vision think about your values in life – if you are going against those with your change, you will without doubt find it more difficult.

All is not lost though - you can have values that are not held dear, but that you need to have to succeed, installed or reordered by a technique that is practised as NLP (neuro linguistic programming), and you can still hold true to your key values.

A true story:

I have never held earning money to be a high value. I worked for years earning far less money than I could have, because I enjoyed the job.

I took a pay cut to spend more time enjoying myself and to be with my parents. I took a pay cut to continue to work in a failing business.

I gave my time away free (as a lot of us do, especially females) when I was in business for myself, so it stopped me earning and achieving my goal.

I had my values assessed and installed money into the mix, which has helped me tremendously - one of my true beliefs is that if you want something enough you can achieve it and you truly have to want it mind, body and soul.

Sometimes your head will rule your heart, sometimes your heart will rule your head, and sometimes something completely unknown gets involved in the mix! When all three are in harmony your goals become easier to achieve.

Some values to consider this is just a list of 18 -- there are over 400!

Accomplishment Achievement Adventure Security Tranquillity Challenge	Wisdom Uniqueness Joy Family Love Certainty	Making a difference Investing Curiosity Creativity Philanthropy Money

If your vision and your goal are creating an environment where you are contradicting your value you will be in conflict with yourself. The first stage to achieving your goal is to recognise the conflict, acknowledge the conflict and do something about it.

On occasions the awareness and acknowledgement resolve the issue for you, and on occasions, as with my money story, it may be such a deeply rooted conflict that you will need external support to adjust it.

External support comes in the form of an intervention, which could include coaching, mentoring, training. The choice is yours.

Vision Board

Creating a vision/mood board can be a useful tool as a screen saver or a wall hanging, and can serve as a source of motivation as you work towards achieving your dreams.

Some people swear by vision boards, so here is a brief description, in case you have never heard of the term before. A vision board is exactly that - it is where you take your vision, whatever that may be, and find pictures, phrases, images, statements that bring your goal to life.

True Story

On my vision board, I have a head with a gold brain with a gold key with a £ symbol on the end dipping into the brain and unlocking it. Beside that I have a picture of a pile of £50 notes, next to that I have a picture of me when I was about 12 kilos lighter, above that I have pictures of my ideal house plus all sorts of other information.

What I have come to realise over time is that I have achieved the pictures that are on the vision board as they are constantly in my sight and in my focus; therefore I achieve them. I have made the vision board far more challenging and aligned to my biggest vision, rather than the smaller vision. Some of the smaller visions have already been achieved.

I do have a written plan and I do direct action toward that plan every day.

Your vision links to your mission and needs to be stated in a positive, and as though you already have it.

> **All of the great achievers of the past have been visionary figures; they were men and women who projected into the future. They thought of what could be, rather than what already was, and then they moved themselves into action, to bring these things into fruition.**
>
> **Bob Proctor**

Factor 4 – Your Strategic Plan (and, yes, you need one)

A strategic plan is the first stage of getting the practicalities of your dream written down in a format that you can do something with. Believe it or not, it works exactly (well very nearly) the same for individuals as it does for businesses.

Plan for the future – with the end in mind
Strategic planning is a process of defining strategy, direction, and making decisions on allocating resources to pursue the strategy. It may also extend to control mechanisms (systems) for guiding the implementation of the strategy. It all sounds a little formal, I know, but there is nothing worse than starting a business, getting a year in and realising that the systems and processes you have put in place are all changing.

This doesn't mean to say that you start off with the system you may need in five years; what it does mean is that you have considered the concept and use the analysis to generate a current decision that will support your future plan and growth easily.

Resources

Key resources you will need are: Time, Money, People, Knowledge and Physical.

Time can be broken down into three areas.

1. Your physical time
2. Others' physical time

3. Time to achieve your goal; what is the deadline?

Money is purely and simply how much you will need to achieve your goal. When calculating finance, remember to include your time as a cost. Outsourcing in the 21st-century when the world is your marketplace can be extremely cost-effective.

You will need finances for;

- Marketing
- Public relations
- Systems
- Staff or outsourcing
- Personal Development your own and others skill sets – training, coaching, mentoring
- Technical equipment and any other equipment required to run your business
- Domain names and web site creation and hosting
- Stock and logistics if you are trading physical product
- Buildings or office space

(Note: this list is not exhaustive, and is dependent on your goal and business)

People are your human resources, and include yourself and your staff team, which may include those that work for you virtually. Staff can be employed or self-employed, full-time or part-time, paid by the job or by the hour, virtual or permanent.

Knowledge can also be intellectual property (IP), and can involve brand, patents, copyrights, trademarks. Include the law required to set up and run a business in whatever country you choose.

Do you have the knowledge or do you bring skilled knowledge in?

Physical covers things such as systems, point-of-sale, buildings, vehicles, any machinery you may need which includes laptops, phones and of course Wi-Fi. Buildings and office space, insurance, personal indemnity, data protection licence.

Strategy

Strategy refers to the objectives and deliberate choices that are made in order to achieve them, such as prioritising certain products and markets. For all of you reading this book who are in the entrepreneurial world or in business for yourself it is your 'niche.'

The more focused you are with your niche, some would say an inch wide and a mile deep, the more focused you can be with any activity to attract your client base.

For those that are reading this as an individual this is the part where you really think about the resources you need, to do whatever it is you are aiming for.

Strategy also refers to the coordination of tasks and activities overall, and the allocation of resources; who does what, which creates a structure so less 'things' fall through the gaps.

A general strategic plan will also include some of the systems you use to get things done. Your strategic plan will clearly indicate if you need staff, if you can outsource the work, or whether it is you doing it all.

The one person band

If you attempt to do everything yourself please ensure you surround yourself with a network of like-minded people. It can be a lonely place working by yourself.

Your strategic planning will also identify the skills and knowledge you may need to achieve your goal, and whether they are locally available.

Mind set without skill set leads to upset

I am a great believer in Mentoring, Coaching, Personal Development, Mastermind groups, Networking and learning activities that grow our awareness and a knowledge base to build and maintain our own businesses. There is a belief that is widely shared that your network is your net worth, and that your earnings will be the average of the 5 people you spend most time with.

It is vital that your vision is clear before you start the plan. The idea is that it will provide you with a systematic approach to achieving successful and sustainable change. This is true whether you are developing this for yourself or for a business.

You will need the ability to lead the change. If you cannot lead yourself and cannot lead others, if you cannot commit to yourself, what will your commitments be like to others?

Timescales – it is never too late to start

Strategic plans generally cover 3, 5 or 10 years and if you consider a legacy think a hundred years into the future. Plans can be longer or shorter, and they can be completed on an annual basis. I would not recommend a year on its own as it is short-term visioning - you need a bigger picture to work from. You will create an annual plan to support the longer strategic plan.

It serves us as individuals to have a 3, 5 and 10 year plan as well. Initially when we are working with goal-setting it can be hard to see beyond the end of next month, but the more we practice developing our future plans the easier it becomes.

It provides us with a bigger picture, that we can communicate regularly to ourselves and to others. We can communicate it to potential funders or business partners and inspire them with our passion, forethought and planning.

It will enable us to set strategic measurements within our plan so we can assess how we are doing and celebrate our success along the way.

The plan is flexible. It can be adjusted. It can be tweaked. Plans are designed to get you to the next stage or the next milestone.

Strategic training – we can be more than we currently are
Along with strategic planning comes strategic training. What this means is that you identify what you need to know and learn to achieve your goal.

You can access training, coaching, mentoring, research; information that meets your needs. Both individuals and businesses will need this training and learning. Change is integral to the achievement of your success; if you are doing something new or something different you will be changing your habits and may need support to keep you on track.

Competence levels

What level of knowledge do you hold currently around the things you need to know, in order to do whatever it is you want to do?

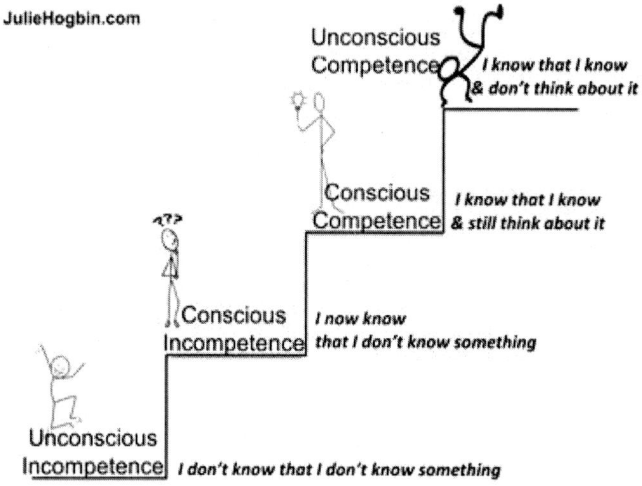

Identify the departments that you need to focus on: marketing, production, sales, finance, personnel, logistics, social responsibility, communication – the list is not endless and each area should be identified as within it there will be specific areas of responsibility and action to be taken.

If you are writing a strategic plan for you as an individual, you will still need to look at things like finance, marketing, staffing and communication. Maybe you are going to do it all yourself but with the potential to leverage and potentially outsource to personal assistants (PAs) or virtual assistants (VAs), or anybody else you can get to help. It's a very similar process for both. It will help you to identify where to focus at any given point in time, and where to spend time, and human and financial capital.

Developing a strategic plan might seem like an overwhelming process, but if you break it down, it's easy to tackle.

As an individual you can, within the strategic plan, identify the philosophies that you want to become your law: certain aspects of your philosophy which you may publish or keep to yourself. It could be part of your branding and your marketing; it can become your individual or organisational published values.

A 9 step approach

1. Be HONEST with yourself or your team
2. Determine the key 'subject' areas that require focus – on your own or with others
3. Research your niche to establish the competitors and customer problems
4. Complete an internal audit on current capabilities in those areas. Team (you)
5. Determine the priority issues; those issues so significant that they require the full and immediate attention of the entire management team (you)
6. Create a plan for each 'subject' area
7. Create a budget and communication plan for each 'subject' area (even if you are in charge of the whole lot)
8. Review, review and review again – schedule regular meetings (even if with yourself) to assess where you are and what you have achieved.
9. Feedback learnings into your plan and keep moving

A strategic plan is a wonderful thing.

Factor 5 - Creating and Writing goals

What is a Goal? The definitions

A definition of goal: An observable and measurable end result having one or more objectives to be achieved within a more or less fixed timeframe.

Dictionary definition and synonyms

1. A pair of posts linked by a crossbar and typically with a net between, forming a space into or over which the ball has to be sent in order to score.

2. The object of a person's ambition or effort; an aim or desired result.
   synonyms: aim, objective, object, grail, holy gril, end, target, design, desire, result, intention, intent, plan, purpose, idea, point, object of the exercise; ambition, aspiration, wish, dream, hope; resolve; raison d'être

I have included the above as you can clearly see whether it is within business, the common dictionary or life in general, when goals are mentioned it is very clearly the same description and intent; getting something completed, in a timeframe, in a direction, with an intent and purpose.

Napoleon Hill talks around the Definiteness of Purpose and this is The Master Key he also talks around our purpose is our earthly destiny and that destiny comes to us when we are ready to see it.

What the mind can conceive and believe the mind can achieve

A classic example of where an individual achieved a goal that everybody else thought was impossible was when Roger Bannister ran the first sub- four-minute mile in 1954 with a time of 3.59.4. He believed in his goal so strongly that he achieved it and set a landmark for future generations. The current record set in 2010 is 3.43.12 held by Hicham el Guerouj.

Even in sport there is a timeframe to be worked to, and measures in place to assess success. These include a league position, medal colours awarded, timings and seed positioning to name just a few.

Inevitability Thinking

Inevitability thinking, made common by Eban Pagen, is thinking and acting as if what you are doing is a foregone conclusion because you set up the conditions for it to happen.

Inevitability thinking is about asking the questions, “How can I make the outcome that I want inevitable?” and “How do I set up the conditions so that the outcome that I want to have happen, happens automatically?”

With inevitability thinking you can set the destination for success and the auto pilot system takes you there. There’s that aviation system again!

Part 1 - View the outcome you want as inevitable

If an outcome becomes inevitable, then the process becomes natural. If success is perceived as inevitable, then you will find a way to make it happen. You are visualising the final result. It already exists. You just have to arrive there.

Part 2 – Creating the conditions

When something is inevitable — it already exists on some level. So you set up the conditions to pull that truth into physical reality.

Conditions directly affect all of your results

Everything you're thinking, every relationship you are in or building, every experience that you have, every team you build, every new product you launch is setting the initial conditions that are going to lead to an outcome.

If you stay conscious of this and pay attention to setting up inevitability conditions, your desired outcomes will start falling into your lap in multiple areas of your life.

> **"If you can tell me who your heroes are, I can tell you how you're going to turn out in life."**
>
> **Warren Buffet**
>
> **"You are an average of the 5 people that you spend the most time with."**
>
> **Jim Rohn**

So how does this link with inevitability thinking – surround yourself with the people who have what you want or who are what you want to be?

Make changes to your life to make his happen – assess your current habits and associations and do what you need to do to be the person who is who they want to be and has what that want to have.

If you hang out with broke, negative people you are probably broke and negative.
If you hang out with wealthy positive people you are either the same or on your way there and you will be positive.

Make a list of five people that you currently know who will bring you closer to living the life you want. These are people who have the qualities that it takes to get where you want to go.

List the five now - if they are not in your immediate circle make a plan

Emma Beck
Julie Hogbin
Rebecca Robertson
Wendy Whittaker-Large
Shirley + David Harwood

If you don't have five extraordinary people in your life to list, start by writing down what the characteristics of those people would be. Be on the lookout for when the opportunity to connect with people of such calibre presents itself, and then, take action.

It is not just about who you spend your time with; equally as important is what you're spending your time doing. All of your activities either improve you or get you closer to your destination, or they take you in the opposite direction.

Life is what happens while you are busy making other plans.

John Lennon

The six stage summary

A summary of where we are so far. Goals are created on a number of levels and in this factor we get into the 'nitty gritty' of how to create them and write them to make sense and create accountability

1. First you create the mission, then the vision or big picture of what you want to do with your life or business. Or within the next 3,5,10, 100 years. This will help identify the large-scale goals that you want to achieve.
2. Secondly, you break the vision down into a strategic plan by subject or area (department, divisions, sections)
3. The strategic plan is then developed for each section to shorter targets, probably annually to start with, that you must hit to reach your lifetime legacy goals.
4. Thirdly you break the year down into six months, three months and monthly, allowing you to check progress and keep on track or adjust as you go.
5. Then you can break the monthly into weekly, daily, hourly if you so desire.
6. Finally, once you have your plan, you start working on it to achieve these goals – the plan becomes a living, breathing document with living, breathing actions.

Initially large goals can be seen as overwhelming; if they are too large – where will you start?

The more you can break the goals down into manageable steps and 'bite sized' chunks the better off you will be to start with, especially if you have never practiced this before.

The more you understand what you are doing, how and when and for what purpose, the better you will be able to express it to others, either as information or to ask for help.

As long as the outcome is clear the process can be adapted; all goals should be adapted to suit. Remember the plane being off track – it happens, it is how we adjust to suit the elements that will lead to our success.

This chapter details two methods you can utilise to support you with your goals. If you utilise the information in this chapter you will be ahead of game – believe me; I have worked with Businesses, Leaders and Entrepreneurs for over two decades, and this is an underutilised and underestimated skill to apply, and one so important for your success

The STRUCTURE Method

S ystem
T arget
R elevant
U nderstand
C ommunicate
T ime
U nderstood
R eview
E valuate

JulieHogbin©

From many years of working with organisations and individuals I have developed my own method of creating well-structured and well written goals with all the key components covered.

System

You need a system to record what is going on and to use for performance review – you really do not want to be scrambling around at a later point attempting to find information on how you or your business are doing.

It will provide you with a story of what has gone on, both as successes and also where you can improve.

If no system exists, be prepared to set aside time to actually monitor response rates and to create a system.

It may be initially a simple filing system which then can be developed into a bigger process – it can be on or offline to start and I would suggest that it ultimately ends up securely online, backed up and forever available.

Target

This is absolutely vital. If you cannot measure it you cannot manage it, review it or evaluate it, and you won't know when you have achieved it.

The other side to this is without a measure you cannot be held accountable by yourself or by others.

Remember the plane is off track up to 95% of the time and it reaches its destination because it knows where it is going; and believe it or not most planes get there within 5 minutes of their programmed arrival time.

Your target MUST have a measure within it, a figure, a percentage, plus or minus, negative or positive, a comparator, a value. Something for you to know it has been achieved or not. All of these are basically around quantity BUT what you also need to think about is how do you measure quality?

Quality is very often described through behaviour such as tone of voice, words used, or through customer polls, reviews, testimonials, feedback, surveys, visible actions such as a smile or eye contact, recording telephone calls for 'training purposes.'

Your measures can become your standards of acceptable performance (SOAP) or your key performance indicators (KPIs).

Relevant

Relevant means that the objective is important to the overarching mission and vision, and you can explain the link.

Relevant to you why are you doing this, what is your driver - this relates back to your originating why. It has to be relevant to you – it has to otherwise you will not do it! It needs to be a deep and burning desire.

Work out why it is relevant to your family, business partner, life partner, joint venture partner, funder, and to anybody else that is involved.

Relevance gains the buy-in when it can be explained and communicated well. It will maintain motivation and enlist people to help you.

This is, one of, your sales tools, and you need to be able to express it in a clearly understood manner, with passion.

Understand

You need to very, very clearly understand why you are doing what you are doing and very, very clearly understand the consequences of you not doing it.

Some of the goals we have can be due to a life or death situation.

I see people every day doing things that will get them closer to a quicker death and they still do them, even when they have been told of the consequences.

Examples are a diabetic sending their sugar levels sky high through eating chocolate on a regular basis, or an alcoholic with liver and kidney damage continuing to drink.

A true story:

A neighbour ignoring the red overdue bills until she was evicted from her home and the house was boarded up.

I often wonder and think about what her goal was. She found the money soon enough to pay the bills but not before her children came home from work and could not get into their home.

Our emotions play a big part of our success. Emotion is 'energy in motion' so remember where your focus goes your energy flows as well. You have limited time and limited energy so make sure you are focusing on the 'right' thing.

Communicate

Communicate, communicate and communicate to all that need to know. This creates understanding for them on what you are doing and what they have to do to support you, or if in business to earn their salary!

It creates accountability for you because you are sharing. When you express your goal to the wide world you are making a commitment verbally that you will achieve it. Remember earlier in the book I wrote about trust and commitment.

It will allow people to ask you questions which will help you to reassess and clarify if you need to – they may ask you a question you hadn't even thought of.

It will allow you to share your passion – the more people know the more they may be able to help you.

Get your message out there to all who will listen – don't bore them, speak with passion. The more you and others hear your message, as long as it is supported by action, you and them will believe it.

Time

When do you want it done by? And how long do you want the task to take?

If the objective is large or project related, the time-based element may require a start date, an end date and ongoing review dates and key milestones.

By agreeing to the dates for milestones or reviews at the start of the objective, the objective owner is clear on what is expected, and by when. If the date is missed the project plan can be adjusted to suit.

Never set the end date with no 'wriggle' room. If something needs to be completed by Friday, set a completion date of Wednesday; then if something unexpected comes up you still have two days to work with. If you get it completed earlier you exceed expectations – both yours and others'.

Some people work far better when under pressure with a deadline looming. What this can mean is that you leave things to the last minute and then scurry around, which can affect the quality.

Time provides you with the urgency of the project and allows you the space to work on the important things with planning.

Be honest with yourself about the time you have. There is nothing worse than setting a goal that is unachievable due to time constraints. With the propensity of humans to 'beat themselves up' over what they have not achieved rather than to look at what they have achieved, do not put yourself in the firing line.

If you are taking on something new, work out in advance how much time you can spend on this new project and set yourself some realistic targets.

Bob Proctor says *'Set a goal to achieve something that is so big so exhilarating that it excites you and scares you at the same time'*

Then you really do need to plan and work out how it fits into your current activities. Proactive operation and planning is required, rather than reactive.

In reality the only thing we can control is our choice on what we do, and when we do it with the time we have available.

> **Results come from doing the right thing, not from doing things right**
>
> **Peter Drucker**

Understood

Your goals and plans need to be understood by others, whether your family, your business partners, your staff team or suppliers, or any other third parties you may be dealing with.

Communication and the relevance of the goal to you and others is key to this understanding.

But you need to really know they do understand so get them (if appropriate) to tell you what they think you said – do it well and it will deepen your relationships.

More importantly you need to understand why you are doing what you are doing. If you do not truly understand and buy into your goal, your unconscious will sabotage your efforts.

Review

If the objective process is not thought through, and resources and constraints not identified, then don't be surprised when you hit a hurdle that could derail you from your original plan.

Regular reviews will clearly identify if you are on track or not before it becomes a disaster – you will be able to do something about it.

Identify resources you will need and review and revise as required. Time is a resource along with many others, as mentioned in an earlier chapter.

If you are working with mentors, accountability partners or business partners, set review dates and review progress.

Evaluate

Evaluate to celebrate success
Evaluate to realign the goal
Evaluate to learn for next time
Evaluate to improve systems
Evaluate to speed the process
Evaluate to deepen relationships
Evaluate to assess finance costs
Evaluate to assess profit margins
Evaluate to reward contribution
Evaluate because you can and see what comes up

Evaluation is used to assess merit, worth and significance using criteria that you have set out through your standards. It will support you in making decisions, gaining insight through reflection for successful practice, and identifying future change.

The SMART Acronym

There is another acronym that you may have heard of called SMART. It is a well-known, although not well-used, applied or understood process. It was spoken about by Peter Drucker in his 1954 book *The Practice of Management.* It certainly has its place, which is why it is in this book.

Peter Drucker wrote about MBO – Managing by Objectives, which in the latter half of the 20th century changed how business organised itself

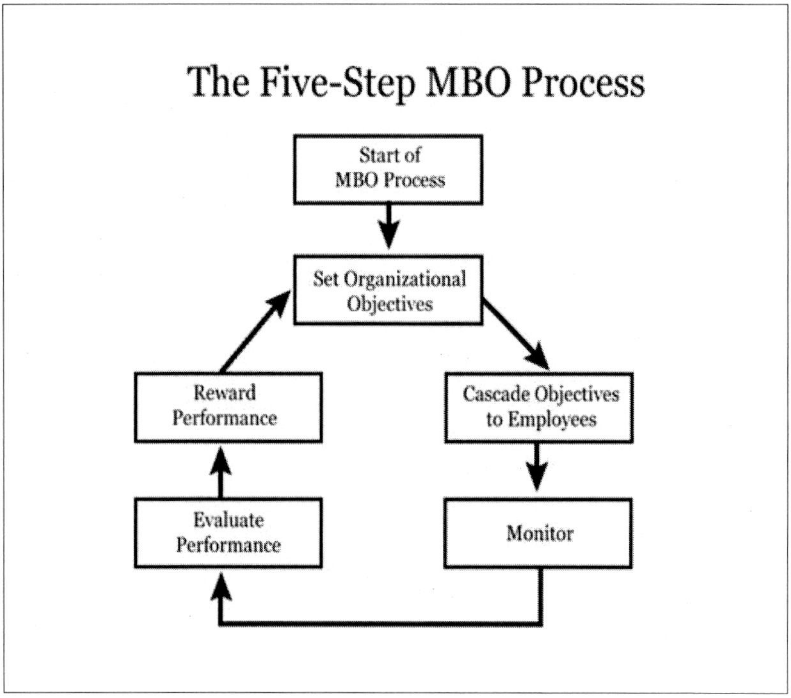

The process, when used well, is a tool to enable you to create specific well thought through and well written goals. It also only described the written format. It does not mention communication, motivation or understanding. Many trainers and writers still use it and will adjust it to suit current working practices – it is definitely a case of 'why reinvent the wheel' and 'if it's not broke don't fix it.'

I have kept this chapter to the original version of SMART as described by Drucker there are adaptations to the model which increase it to SMARTer – the er can stand for evaluate and rewrite or emotionally resilient. Work with whatever works with and for you. It is a flexible model, when you truly understand it, and remember there is always more than one way to do anything! The STRUCTURE model is a great alternative that provides a broader perspective on what is required.

SMART was written specifically to manage by objectives within a business setting. Goals can be given to you through a hierarchy to achieve somebody else's goal or chosen by you to achieve your goal.

SMART as a method doesn't really allow for those big exhilarating and exciting goals that scare you. SMART fits very nicely when you are in the day-to-day activities required in the daily, weekly, monthly, or quarterly plan.

Examples

Following are a few simple examples of smaller goals generated to fulfil the vision; you will create your own linked to your own vision.

Area: Wealth

1. Why: To create a pension for my retirement
2. Vision: I own 20 houses each with a net profit of 1k a month

    1. Goal: Learn business skills
        1. Research appropriate providers generating a list of providers by 6pm on the 25th of this month
        2. Book calls to connect with the provider by noon on the 26th of this month

2. Goal: Increase my network
    1. Research the local networking events to attend (by time day month year) by 2pm Thursday the 25th
    2. Attend two meets a week for the next 4 weeks
    3. At each event attended meet 5 new connections
    4. Follow up with the 5 connections made within 48 hours of the meet

3. Goal: Research and select area for investment
    1. Complete due diligence (by time day month year)
    2. Walk the streets (by time day month year)
    3. Visit the agents (by time day month year)

4. Goal: To Generate Leads through leafletting direct to vendor
    1. Design a leaflet (by time day month year)
    2. Research printers (by time day month year)
    3. Select printer and send PDF for printing (by time day month year)

5. Goal: To recruit & select a leaflet delivery person (by time day month year
    1. Do the first delivery with them to establish standards (by time day month year)
    2. First 1000 leaflets to be delivered (by time day month year)
    3. Second 1000 leaflets to be delivered (by time day month year)

Setting an objective that requires 'leaflets to be delivered' is not good enough. 'Deliver 2000 leaflets Friday the 4th between 10am and 1pm' is much better. You also need a system, standards and KPIs, in place to measure whether this is being achieved.

Specific	In the context of developing objectives specific means that we describe an observable action, behaviour or achievement that is also linked to a measure, number percentage or frequency.
Measurable	A measure is a method or procedure that allows the assessment of the behaviour or action on which the objective is focused. It may well be a number or % either positive or negative, a £ figure; all described here are as a quantity. You will also want to think about how do you measure quality? Another aspect of measure is that you need to clearly be able to say the goal has been met, allowing for celebration.
Achievable	People need to be capable of achieving the goals set for them. There needs to be a good likelihood of success. However, achievable does not mean easy or simple. Effective objectives need to be stretching. Setting objectives that are plainly unrealistic does not motivate and people will apply little energy or enthusiasm to a task that is futile. Resources should be considered.
Realistic	It is important to evaluate your situation honestly and recognise which goals are realistic and which are a little far-fetched. Ask yourself if you have all the things you need to complete your goal, such as skill, resources, time, knowledge.
Timebound	Somewhere in the objective there needs to be a date. The date needs to specify a day, month and year. Research around what type of goals motivate shows that a specific date '31 August 20**' is far more motivating than a vague goal such as 'by the end of August'. It is useful to include a time as well, especially if you are working with others.

Setting a goal to attend one networking meeting in the next month is not a good one. Setting a goal to attend one networking meeting in the next month and stay until the end may be a huge and scary goal if you are really not happy with being in a group you do not know.

Setting a goal to attend one Angel Networking meeting in the next month may be huge if you never have and not so if you have high net worth Individuals in your circle

Each goal you set will promote different feelings within you dependent on your level of comfortableness with the subject matter.

More on the comfort zone later.

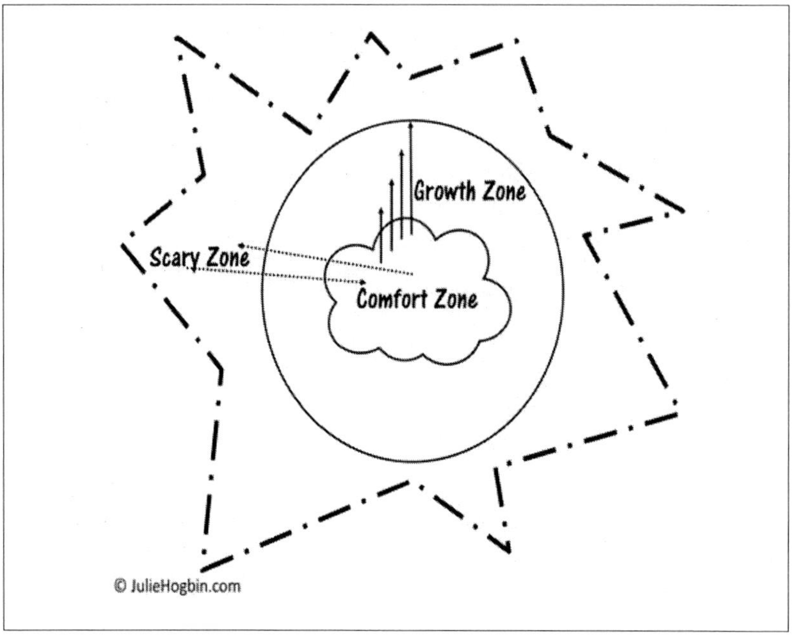

Area: Philanthropy

1. Why: To make the world a better place
2. Vision: I have donated 200k to charity
    3. Goal: To run a sponsored marathon in September 20xx
        1. Take one exercise class a week on Wednesday at 7am.
        2. Buy an exercise bike on Friday evening this week.
        3. Build up my mileage by adding a mile a week to my distance

    4. Goal: To raise sponsorship of a minimum £5,000 for September 20xx
        1. Investigate the sponsorship platforms to use by 31 January 20xx

2. Register with the chosen marathon organisers on 14 February 20xx
3. Select the charity I wish to run for by 10 January 20xx

'I am going to walk more' is far more difficult to measure than 'Every day I am going to walk around the block 16 times.'

'I am going to buy 4 types of green vegetables each shop' is better than 'I am going to buy more vegetables.'

Now practice writing some for yourself or your business – contact me if you are having difficulty – remember this is a skill that has to be learnt and practiced to improve it.

All goals have their parameters, set by the person writing them, and each and every one of you is different in your knowledge, your strengths, your courage etc. It serves us well to remember that and not compare one for one without first finding out the background of others.

As someone once said, "What are we comparing, apples with apples or oranges with lemons?"

Start writing your goals now the more practice you get the easier it becomes

Factor 6 - Communicating our Goals Effectively

The context of communication

Communication is such a simple word, but it describes one of the most complex functions of our nature as human beings.

We will communicate with each other in a variety of ways and in this wonderful 21st century communication can be face to face and more often than not we communicate through other means:

- E-mails (and most of us have more than one address)
- Facebook
- Twitter
- LinkedIn
- Text messaging
- Over the phone
- Whats app
- Skype
- Pinterest
- Instagram
- Snapchat
- And more recently a surge of marketing through the post! & the list goes on

The majority of our communication in today's world is not face to face - the art of conversation is dying unless we want to communicate and learn how to do it effectively.

A whole range of subtleties comes into play, especially when we are working in deficit of not being face to face, and even that can be difficult at times.

Communicating well, involves more than just the written or spoken word; that is only one small part of our language.

Body language, our tone of voice, accent, and speed of speech play a huge part in our delivering the message well or not, as the case may be.

The Complete Picture - Gestalt theory

As humans we want the complete story. If we do not receive it, what do we do? We make something up in order to make the story whole. We are hardwired to complete the picture.

Gestalt psychology identified the principle of closure. This refers to the mind's tendency to see complete figures or forms even if the picture is incomplete, partially hidden by other objects, or if part of the information needed to make a complete picture in our minds is missing.

The Gestalt theory focuses on the mind's perceptive processes, and the theorists followed the basic principle that the whole is greater than the sum of its parts. In viewing a part, a cognitive process takes place and the mind takes a leap to making up the rest and creating the whole.

Gestalt theory seeks completeness; when shapes aren't closed we tend to add the missing elements to complete the image. Our minds, our perception, completes the shape and closure occurs.

What do you see in the pictures? The pictures on either end are not complete but we will see a complete picture and make it recognisable to something we think we know.

The middle picture is an old favourite, and dependent on how you view it you will see one of two images. Some people are never able to see both even when it is pointed out to them. It is all a matter of perception.

Closure is also thought to have evolved from ancestral survival instincts, in that if one was to partially see a predator their mind would automatically complete the picture and know that it was a time to react to potential danger even if not all the necessary information was readily available

Let me ask you a question. How many times have you spoken to somebody on the phone and when you get to meet them, they look nothing like the picture you have in your head?

How many of you have watched some words appear in the feed on Facebook and make a snap decision on whether you like or dislike the individual that is posting the message?

How many of you receive a written message and think "What are they shouting about?"

We do it both consciously and unconsciously. Part of the joy of learning around communication (which will be the next book in detail) is that we can choose to communicate well and effectively to deliver our message in whatever format we choose.

We communicate both externally and internally. We communicate with yourself and with others.

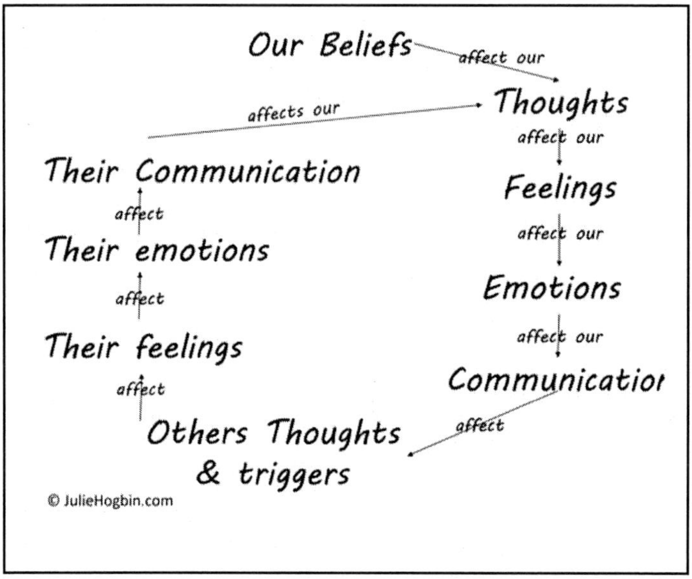

We are always affecting others by how we interact; we are 'emotionally contaging' them, so to speak.

To effectively communicate, anything, we need to manage the whole process. If we get a reaction that we were not expecting, we need look to assess our language and actions.

***'Seek to understand before being understood.' ***

Internal Communication – our inner voice

So what does your communication with yourself have to do with achieving your goals? Believe it or not, our unconscious is what drives our behaviours, and the primary role of your unconscious is to keep you safe. Our unconscious is our fight, flight, freeze mechanism.

You can have the greatest mission, the best vision, an incredibly detailed and perfect plan with wonderful well-written goals that you have expressed to the world, but if your unconscious believes you are putting yourself into a dangerous position it will sabotage you at every opportunity it gets.

When you are in alignment with your purpose, and your unconsciousness believes you and you can assure it that you will keep it safe, it will support you in every way it can.

Internal communication is where we speak to ourselves. It's that little voice in our head. It's that little voice - the one that just spoke to you when I asked you a question!

We need to manage the little voice, which comes from our belief systems, value systems and our unconscious. It will repeat back to us what we have heard in the distant past and what it thinks we want to hear.

Our subconscious keeps us safe in its own right, and sometimes when our subconscious, does its job and, perceives it is keeping us safe, it keeps us in our comfort zone. You need to convince your unconscious that you are doing something that you truly believe in and that you believe you deserve.

If it perceives we are looking to go into a 'danger' zone the little voice will kick in to tell us to stay safe. We need to train our little voice into our new way of being in the world if we want to achieve our goals.

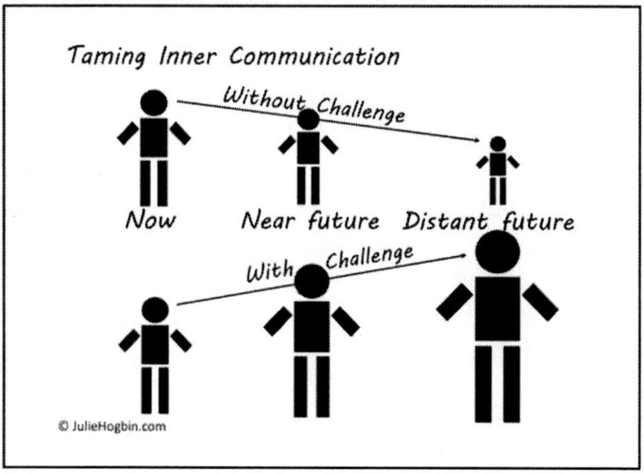

If we are not growing we are stagnating and minimising ourselves; we are not living to our true potential. Some say we are dying (which actually is true) – think of grass without water, think of hay making without sunshine, think of children without adventure.

As children we do not have the fears we have as adults. We do not have the inner voice telling us to be careful, to look after ourselves, to not do that because it will make us unsafe. We have not been told that we can't, we have not been told that our dreams are unrealistic; that happens as we get older and are exposed to other influences from education, to the media, to our peer group and many other sources.

If as children we did have that inner voice would we ever have learned how to walk? Think about how many times you fell over? As a child learning to ride your first bike how many times did you fall off or wobble? Did it stop you? For some it probably did and for others it most certainly didn't and it will still have the same effect now.

A true story:

When I fell off my bike as a child and hit my head on the curb, whilst I was learning to ride without stabilisers, my inner voice (& I remember it well) said "Stay off and push it home; this is dangerous and you have hurt yourself, and you will do it again."

My father's external voice said "Get back on the bike; if you don't now you probably never will." With the love and trust I held for my father, I got back on that bike and didn't look back. It made all the difference.

My own inner voice was quietened by someone I trusted who had greater experience than me - In that instance my father became my mentor.

People affect you all the time with how they influence you; it is your job to question and challenge that impact.

You have the goals you want to achieve – your inner voice will challenge you and sabotage you along the way even if the goal is a positive one. It is change you are aiming for.

Your job is to recognise your inner voice, thank it and not let it stop you. The more 'it' realises you are safe, responsible enough, sensible enough and that you will look after yourself, the more it will accept the new way.

External Communication

What message are you putting out into the world when you communicate your goals?

Your external communication is far more than the physical words you speak, especially not when emotions are involved.

Your body language and what you sound like make up the other part of the message. You use the facial expressions and mannerisms, the tone of your voice, the speed you speak at, and the accent you have.

All add or detract from the message that you are aiming to deliver.

The words you write and how you write them are so important, as are the pictures you create. As humans we are hardwired to make a complete story of any piece of information we receive. We subjectively add to the information we receive to make it a whole rather than a part.

We have to objectively assess the information that comes into our realm of consciousness. When we deliver it, we need to be conscious of the effect we are having on others.

You cannot know what filters others are hearing or seeing your words through, whether they be written or spoken. You cannot know what upbringing, education or emotions they are experiencing whilst you are talking to them. You cannot know what interpretation they have of a word you use – as they don't of you. You cannot know what trigger you are pushing! All you know is what you can physically see in front of you.

The majority of us are not psychologists, trained in the art of reading people. Some of us who have worked within the people industry for decades can make a very good guess at what is happening with people; we learn how to read others.

All we can do is be as clear and as objective as we possibly can, with the message we are delivering.

So what does this mean?

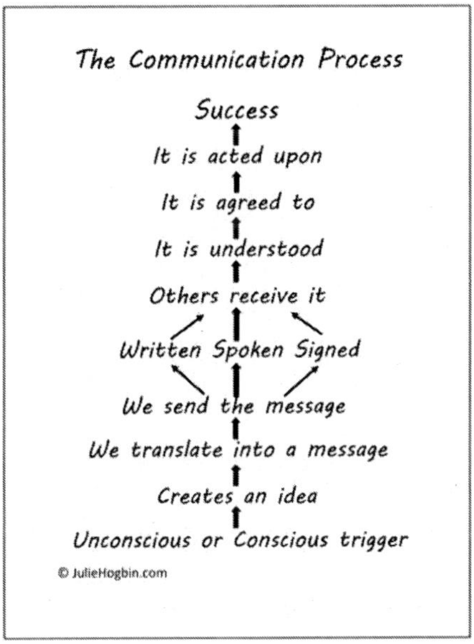

Externally you need to express your passion for the subject and not let that passion get in the way of the message; you need to be concise without using too many words.

Too many words confuse and if you confuse them you lose them or at the least they will stop listening.

You need to have practised what you are going to say, so that it sits very comfortably with you saying it. If it does not sit comfortably with you, those paying attention will hear it and see it in your communication. In general, people believe what they see rather than what they hear. You need to be in alignment with yourself and your message; you need to be congruent with what you express.

Fact: Brains function far faster than we can speak so don't be surprised when people lose interest in what you are saying!

It is said most of us speak at the rate of about 125 words per minute. However, we have the mental capacity to understand someone speaking at 400 plus words per minute.

This difference between speaking speed and thought speed means that when we listen to the average speaker, we're using only 25 percent of our mental capacity. We still have 75 percent to do something else with.

They will be mentally shopping, creating the next presentation, talking to themselves internally – you have to be as interesting and as attractive as you can be to keep their attention.

What it doesn't mean is that we can speak more words to fill the space or speak too much faster.

When you express your goal(s) you have to somehow gain others' buy in to your vision. The parable detailed below is a very good example of how a vision and a mission can change people's views and enjoyment of what they are doing – yours included.

The Parable of the Three Stonecutters

Once upon a time, a traveller came across three stonecutters and asked them what they were doing.

The first replied saying that he was the most miserable person on Earth and that he has the hardest job in the world. "Every day I have to move around huge stones make a living, which is barely enough to eat." The traveller gave him a coin and continued walking.

The second one did not complain and was focused on his work. When the traveller asked him what he was doing, the stonecutter replied "I'm earning a living by doing the best job of stonecutting in the entire county. Although, the work is hard, I'm satisfied with what I do and I earn enough to feed my family." The traveller praised him, gave him a coin and went on.

When the traveller met the third stonecutter, he noticed that the stonecutter cutter had sweat and dust on him but he looked happy and was singing a cheerful song. The traveller was astonished and asked "What are you doing?" The stonecutter looked up with a visionary gleam in his eye and said, "Can't you see? I am building a Cathedral."

Foresight – if only we could see into the future

Goals are forward focused, and you cannot guarantee what will happen. All you can do is do what you can, as well as you can, with what you have and what you can get.

Do you have a crystal ball? I know some of you will. Whether you believe in predictions or not, planning and action are the key to creating your future.

Putting yourself in the right place, with the right people, at the right time will enhance your opportunities – without any doubt.

You create your own world in which to operate. Unfortunately a 2013 study discovered that greater belief in precognition was held by those who felt low in control, and that the belief can act as a psychological coping mechanism.

This means that if you do not feel as though you have the power and are in control, you give up your future as being something you cannot do anything about – you end up accepting 'your lot' in life.

NO – that is just not true! You cannot be held responsible for your start in life, but over a certain age every decision you make affects your results, and for that you can only hold yourself responsible.

We all start from where we start, with what we have. Some of the greatest stories are about people who had nothing and amass fortunes, or who were persecuted and change the world.

> **The only person you are destined to become is the person you decide to be.**
>
> **Ralph Waldo Emerson**

It is all about the choices you make and the belief you have in yourself. A question I will ask you is, who affects your belief in yourself?

Write a list of those that:	
Positively affect you	Negatively affect you

Hindsight – is a wonderful thing if we do something with it

> Life can only be understood backwards, but it must be lived forwards.
>
> Soren Kierkegaard

You can all with hindsight assess and learn from your previous actions if you choose to!

The definition of insanity, as made famous by Einstein, is 'doing the same thing over and over and over again and expecting a different result!' He also said 'We cannot solve our problems with the same thinking we used when we created them.'

Two key lessons to be taken from those statements;

1. Do things differently and
2. Change your thinking

And it is not quite as easy as writing the words in this book. As the adult you are, you have a lifetime of experiences and living life to adjust. You have arrived at this point in your life – and for some of you where you are is OK. That is what sometimes causes you an issue – you are OK, you are comfortable, why on earth would you rock the boat?

What is your driver to change - you can simply carry on!

BUT you are reading this book for a reason – even if you don't really know what it is yet.

Adult learning

Adult learning and change basically needs four things to be considered, explained or challenged to succeed:

1. Timing

a. The urgency of doing something NOW and you need to understand and accept the NOW
b. Adults tend towards a problem - solving approach and like things that have the ability to be actioned immediately
c. The quicker you put new knowledge into practice the more you will remember (get writing those goals)

2. Self-Concept

a. Adults are more willing to trust their own judgement
b. Ideas that conflict with values and held beliefs will take far longer to accept and may never be thought useful

3. Experience

a. You have a large resource to tap into that you are proud of
b. New learning, if associated to current knowledge, is retained more easily
c. Learning that relates to short - term memory is harder to remember

4. Motivation

a. Adults learn best when actively involved at their own pace
b. With material suited to them – one size does not fit all
c. Learning is related to phases in your life – why now?
d. Learning is related to social roles and it causes pleasure

What does this mean? You trust yourselves because you have your life as testament to your survival – anything that jars or clashes with your belief systems and moral compass will be questioned and may not be believed, and therefore not actioned.

Interestingly, that will not just be from others – it will be from you as well. If you are choosing to take a path that your previous experiences have shied away from or somebody has taught you is 'wrong' the ability to learn and put into practice will be severely restricted.

A classic example of this is when you are in business for yourself and want to run a profitable growth - driven organisation so that you can live a life of luxury or even have money in the bank for a 'rainy' day.

If you have been bought up to believe that:

- 'Money is the root of all evil'
- 'Rich people are nasty, slimy, backstabbing individuals'
- 'You have to work hard to make money'
- * 'Money doesn't buy happiness'

How do you think you will do at earning the money and then keeping it? With these programs running through our unconscious it will be far harder to achieve our goal.

We are conditioned at a very young age to believe certain things and to behave in a certain way. It happens at an unconscious level through the influences that are around us – we copy the behaviours, thought processes and verbal commands we receive from those that we are surrounded by. Our parents, teachers, siblings, peer group, media ....

All of these things are who we are today, and drive our every action and behaviour, more often than not without us understanding that.

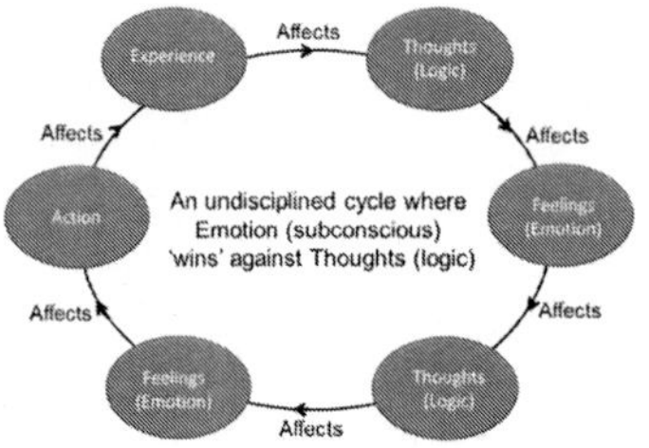

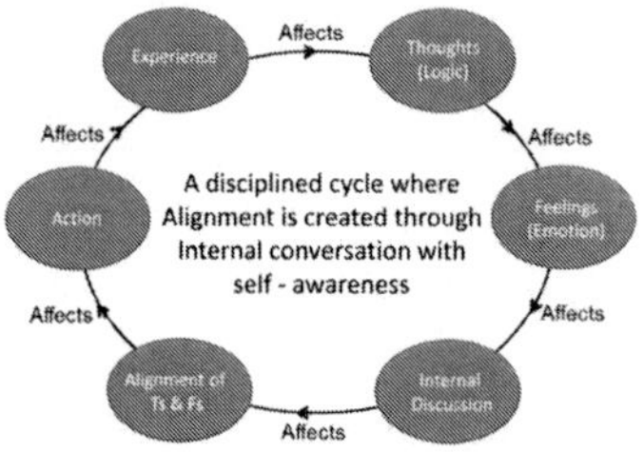

Unfortunately when the subconscious mind must choose between deeply rooted emotions and logic (goal setting) the emotions will almost always win.

But all is not lost. All of your subconscious thoughts, programs and conditioning can be 'repaired' if you choose to, by first becoming aware of what is going on for you and then secondly doing something about it.

One part of this book will not result in the results you wish for. The information contained needs to internalised and worked through at the conscious, pre conscious and unconscious levels.

If you refer to the wheel of life you will recognise where the most work needs to be completed and which parts of you need work.

Everything is possible with a goal, with a plan, with awareness and with change

Factor 7 - What gets you to the result or not as the case may be!

Motivation – what is it really?

Whatever your reason, you have made it your goal to buy this book – something piqued your interest.

Not only did you buy it; you are reading it – so somewhere consciously or unconsciously you have taken actions to achieve your goal and you have recognised that you need to know more about setting goals to achieve change and more success.

Were the goals thought through or made on the spur of the moment? Something motivated you to do what you did that got you to this point!

What influenced you?

A definition of motivation that I have worked with for over two decades is:

> ***Motivation is a conscious or unconscious driving force that arouses and direct action towards the achievement of a desired goal***

I love it and have never found, generated or read one that is any better or covers motivation in its entirety as this one does.

The definition indicates that motivation can be both a conscious or unconscious action and process. Think about the way you do what you do, your behaviours and thoughts. Some will be conscious decisions you make and some will be completely unconscious, where you operate through your developed habits.

Where do habits come from? They may be developed over years, inherited or we may have only just started them – with the influences we have around us in everyday life and the peer pressure we experience new habits are started with us being unconsciously aware.

Think about the advent of Starbucks/Nero or Pret – do you now regularly get a coffee on the way to work when you never used to, or do you know people who do?

Think about the advent of phones with storage for audio – do you now regularly watch or listen to music or film on the way to work when you never used to, or do you know people who do?

Sometimes we operate in a completely unconscious way. Some simple examples for you to consciously think about and then you can start to think of yours for yourself:-

Think about how you cross the road; do you unconsciously adopt the behaviours that get you safely to the other side? As children you were probably taught to look, left, right and left again (I am based in the UK), to check for oncoming traffic, but as adults you do not consciously think about that; you just do it. When you travel to another road system you consciously need to change to think right, left, right – how many times have you nearly walked out in front of traffic because unconsciously you have reverted to habit?

How many of you have ever driven from A to B and don't really remember how you got there? You have arrived safely, maybe with luck, from an unconscious set of actions.

Think about how you breathe. It is an unconscious action for us, unless something happens to make breathing difficult – then and only then do you really ever think about it.

Now let's look at this from a conscious aspect. Sometimes you need to think about what you are doing - this is where your conscious thought kicks in.

Something triggers a thirst in you so you consciously make the decision to find the liquid that in that moment is what you fancy. The conscious decision is to get a drink and it may be a conscious or an unconscious decision as to which one you choose.

You are planning a travel trip and you have choices to make about whether you go by plane, train, car or bus. You will make a conscious choice based on what is right for you at that time, or which fits your time or budget.

I am continuously making conscious choices about the content of this book – nothing is unconscious as this is the first I have written.

The Motivation definition indicates that motivation is a driving force that arouses and directs action - what does this mean? For me it indicates power and energy that creates movement to do something. It is up to you what that something is!

And the last piece - the achievement of a desired goal - very simply means we want the 'thing' whatever that may be.

Everything you do is goal driven: everything you do is because you want the end result – whatever that end result or behaviour may be!

> A couple of examples:
>
> A child at the checkout in a supermarket has been told they cannot have any sweets so they start to perform and have a tantrum. What's motivating the child is that they know by creating all this fuss, their parent will buy the sweets to quieten them – it is a learnt behaviour from the child to achieve their goal.
>
> Think about the goal of the parent.
>
> You come home from work with the intent of finishing a report that is due in the morning and instead you take a bottle of wine from the fridge and sit in front of the TV all night, watching anything that flits across the screen. What is the motivation here? Is it that you really want to watch the soaps but won't admit it to yourself, is it that you just want to sit and do nothing, staring blankly into space, or is it that you know you will have the attention of the person that the report is for when you miss the deadline?
>
> What goal are you achieving by sitting in front of the TV with a bottle of wine?

You have your why, and your vision and mission are complete. You have your plan, your goals are written down and you have told others what you are aiming to do.

But you still don't achieve your desired outcomes - is this resonating with you?

What stops you?

Basically it is because you do not want the change enough and are not prepared to do what it takes. You self-sabotage and doubt yourself.

Some familiar reasons that I have heard and some I have personal experience of;

- The comfort of carrying on doing what we have already done.
- The fear of doing something different
- The why isn't strong enough
- There's always tomorrow
- So and so won't like it
- You face opposition from your partner, friend, parents, siblings etc
- Feeling silly
- Thinking others will laugh at you
- Scared of standing out
- Going against the norm
- It's hard
- It's the unknown
- You haven't done it before
- You just can't be bothered
- You truthfully like how you are
- Someone else has told you to
- You think you are not worth it
- You are scared of success
- You are scared of making a mistake
- It is all too difficult
- Entrenched habits

> *There are seven days in the week and someday isn't one of them!*

Really think about what it is that stops you; be honest with yourself – you will be the only person who truly knows. Once you have identified it you can work with it and do something about it – tick the above list if you think they apply to you and add to it if you think of more.

Add your own inhibitors here and be honest with yourself - in truth it is only you who knows what is stopping you others will only be able to guess.

Abraham Maslow's Hierarchy of Needs

There are many, many different models of motivation to choose from, and I add Maslow to this book as it bears relevance when you are looking to possibly shake the foundations of your world! Maslow focused on what goes right with people; he was interested in human potential, and how we fulfil that potential.

I have added my knowledge to the model as I have learnt over the decades that certain patterns emerge when 'things' change. It is certainly worth considering when you are thinking about what is going on for you in achieving your goals.

Maslow is known for claiming that human beings are motivated by unsatisfied needs, and that lower needs have to be met before higher needs can be satisfied.

He also said that if a lower level need is 'rattled' we will retreat to the lower level to satisfy that level before we can continue at the higher level. The original piece of work was completed and published in the 1940's & 1950's.

According to Maslow, there are four general types of needs at the lower levels of the model - physiological, safety, love/belonging, esteem - and they must be satisfied before a person can act unselfishly or in Maslow's words, self-actualise. Only when these are satisfied can the individual transcend and look outside of self.

Maslow called these needs "deficiency needs." As long as you are motivated to satisfy these cravings, you are moving towards growth and self-actualisation.

When one deficiency need is met, a higher need emerges. When this in turn is satisfied, again new and still higher needs emerge, and so on. As one desire is satisfied, another pops up to take its place.

Satisfying these needs is natural and healthy to do, and if one need that was met is 'shaken' then you will descend back to the shaken level to make it right before ascending the hierarchy once again.

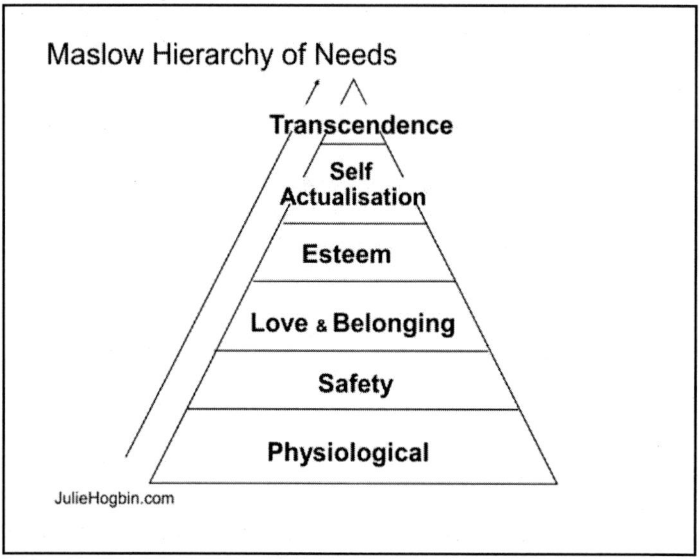

1st Level Physiological Needs

Physiological needs are the very basic needs such as air, water, food, warmth, sleep, sex, shelter, etc. When these are not satisfied we may feel sickness, irritation, pain, discomfort, and so on.

These feelings motivate us to alleviate them as soon as possible to regain our equilibrium. Once they are alleviated, we can start to think about other areas.

Think about when you are sitting in a training session or cannot get to food or liquid and you are hungry or thirsty – the minute you realise it (for most of us) your whole being focuses on that need. Your concentration wavers, your inner voice starts talking to you. If you are in a basement room without windows for a long period of time you will start to crave natural light and fresh air.

A classic example: When you have an office move I guarantee you will have people whose main concern becomes where their parking space is, the positioning of their desk and chair, and who gets the window.

This level should never be underestimated as it is your basic driver.

2nd Level Safety Needs

Safety needs have to do with establishing stability and consistency in a chaotic world. These needs are mostly psychological in nature. They are about having a sense of security and feeling protected from danger.

If the hairs on the back of your neck go up when you are in the presence of someone or you get a gut feeling that something isn't right – take note. This is your basic survival process kicking in to warn you.

In a working environment this is all to do with knowing the processes and systems of how the organisation works, and can be as basic as "How do I book a day's annual leave?" or "When can I leave my desk?".

3rd Level Love Needs

Love and belongingness are your social needs. Humans have a desire to belong to groups: clubs, work groups, religious groups, family, gangs, networks etc. You, believe it or not, crave human interaction. You need to feel loved by others, to be accepted by others and to belong.

We are naturally pack animals and will follow a leader – for most of us we will need to learn how to stand out from the 'crowd'

> **If your goal means you leave a group that has provided you with your love needs – find another group that provides you with replacement love, otherwise you will crave the need and it will hinder your higher growth.**

4th Level Esteem Needs

There are two types of esteem needs.

1st is self-esteem, which results from competence or mastery of a task and could be labelled cognitive, which is gaining of knowledge and giving meaning to your life, focused around mastery of a skill.

Attention - seeking behaviour is common in those with low self - esteem

2nd is status, which we achieve when others give us attention, recognition and appreciation. In a working environment look for how people get hung up on role titles.

> ***I have seen adults behave just like children at the checkout looking for sweets when trying to gain the attention of someone in power.***

How do you get your status and esteem needs met currently? And if you change what you do, how will you get this level met?

Within this level as well is our aesthetic needs, in regard to an appreciation of and search for beauty.

5th Level Self-Actualisation

The need for self-actualisation is "the desire to become more and more what one is, to become everything that one is capable of becoming." People who have their other needs met can maximize their individual potential; they seek growth, personal development, achievement, self-fulfilment and peak experiences.

Transcendence needs

Simply put – transcendence needs involve helping others to achieve self-actualisation. This is where you serve a higher goal outside of self. This is where individuals will become mentors, coaches, or trainers and give back to the world – it doesn't mean they don't do this earlier but at this point it becomes a burning desire.

These needs spring from the depths of our common life as human beings. They may attract us to, or repel us from, any given group.

Consider the goals you are looking to set and recognise if you are rattling the lower levels – if you are then bear this in mind when you start to falter and focus on repairing the level that has been rattled.

Habits – Yes we are a big one!

You will be learning and looking to change habits, even if you do not realise it just yet. So how do you adopt a new habit to make it stick?

Firstly let's look at what a habit is.

A habit is an acquired pattern of behaviour that often occurs automatically and unconsciously through repetition

Psychologists say "It is a behaviour that is repeated, which is generally unconscious. A habit is a more or less a fixed way of thinking and behaving, and becomes routine for those that are demonstrating the behaviour."

What is interesting is that habits are often unknown by the person exhibiting the behaviour. The habit becomes routine and unless you are willing to engage in self-analysis, requesting feedback with the intent of creating self-awareness, you will be unaware that you are exhibiting that habit. Even when you know what it is you do that stops you or holds you back, it can be difficult to change as the habit is comfortable to you!

Your habits will come from your subconscious, as habits are things we do without thinking. Realising this and thinking about what you've already read throughout the book, how will you raise your level of awareness on what you will be facing when you choose your new goals?

Have you ever tried to change a habit? Some of the common ones that spring to mind are your diet, biting nails, smoking, drinking, and fitness. Let me add some more; saying yes when you mean no! Not saying what you know you should, writing a plan and then not sticking to it.

Do you set New Year's resolutions? Do you achieve them? Or do you get two weeks into the year and you are back to doing what you have always done?

A piece of research was completed in 2010 (Phillippa Lally, Cornelia van Jaarsveld, Henry W. W. Potts & Jane Wardle) which found the average time for participants to reach the 'asymptote of automaticity' was 66 days, with a range of 18–254 days

So it takes a minimum of 18 days of doing something before you create a new habit with an average of 66 and for some much longer at 254 days!

Just this one piece of research clearly indicates that we are all different, and new habits can take a while to form. Think about how different the 'thing' is that you want to do from what you are already doing, and then think about how you feel about the change.

Habits can be good or bad (in whose eyes, I ask?), are sometimes compulsory and sometimes caused through more complex issues. I am referring to mental health and addictions.

One key factor in distinguishing a habit is whether the person can control the behaviour.

I wake up to a visible quote which says:

> **'Every morning I have two choices – I can continue to sleep with dreams or wake up and chase my dreams – the choice is mine'**
>
> **I wake up and chase my dreams. What do you do?**

> **A goal is a dream with a deadline**
>
> **Napoleon Hill**

I choose my behaviours, and choose to control them so I am self-aware (with a little help from others).That way, I can create new habits and ways of being. Some are easier than others to adopt, some I resist for longer but I get here in the end by breaking things down into manageable chunks and practice to create repetition, creating new success habits.

To create new habits you need to challenge your own unconscious set of behaviours. This involves stopping doing things which are comfortable, which are easy, which are known. To create a habit that will be different, unknown, not the norm, you have to think about. until it becomes, through repetition, part of your unconscious processes and your new habit.

It has been said that we are 90% habit! This means that, from the time we wake up to the time we go to sleep we are operating within an unconscious framework. We do 100s and probably 1,000s of things in the same way, at the same time, on a daily, weekly, monthly, yearly routine.

A simple exercise

Clasp your hands together as you would normally, without thinking about it. Look to see how you have your hands - it may be left over right, right over left, or fingers entwined. Check your thumb positions and feel how comfortable it is.

Now reverse everything; do everything you have done the other way round - How does that feel?

Pretty uncomfortable, I expect?

Unclasp your hands, shake them about a little and then clasp them together again.

Which way have you done it?

I bet the greater majority of you have gone back to exactly the way you always do this as it is comfortable - it is your habit.

Another simple one to try is your washing routine in the morning - do it in a different order - the last time I did this I ended up confused as to what had been completed and what hadn't! An odd experience which I had to smile at.

My morning is my inspirational and thinking time for the day and I had put myself out of routine and order. Changing one habit automatically threw another one into disarray without me realising it would.

Why do you operate within the habit based routine? Purely and simply because you are bombarded, there is so much information, there is so much to do, there are so many things going on around you that you have to; conscious thought is hard in terms of energy consumption whereas habit is not.

Think about when you are really paying attention, concentrating and listening to learn – how tired are you at the end of the session? I expect very tired is the answer, as it is not the norm for most people.

> **Perseverance is the hard work you do after you get tired of doing the hard work you already did.**
>
> **Newt Gingrich**

Filtering all of that information consciously is hard in terms of energy consumption. On the other hand it is easy to develop a set of habits that cater to our perceived needs. They take less energy and thought to execute. Over the years we develop a set of entrenched habits that determine how well we succeed in every area of our life.

If you are looking to change things it will first help to think about how long you have been demonstrating that way of behaving - how old you are and how self-aware you are and whether your habits have been entrenched for many years.

The longer the habit has been in place the harder it will be to change – break it down and celebrate small successes on route to your end goal.

One of the issues is that your habits, driven by your unconscious, create your comfort zone.

The Comfort Zone

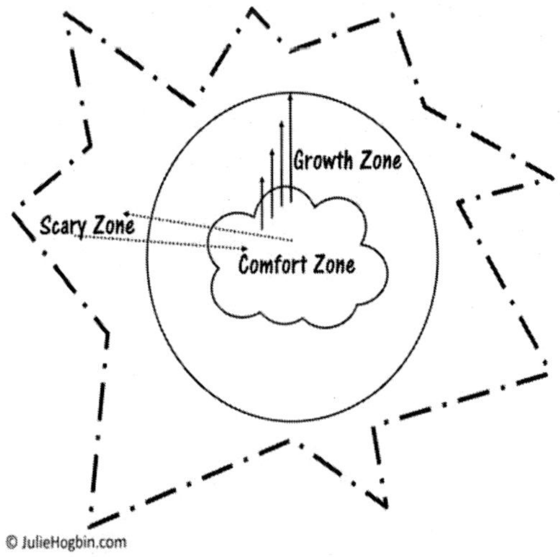

The comfort zone is a place or a situation where you feel safe and at ease. It provides you with a settled method of working that requires little effort and does not stretch you.

It is said that "If you stay within your comfort zone you will never improve."

The comfort zone can be described as 'a behavioural state where a person operates from an anxiety-neutral position.'

It is where you operate and are comfortable; you know what to do and how to do it. It is easy, warm and fluffy.

You are in control or at least you feel you are. You are safe, certain and secure.

The only way to grow and develop is to come out of your comfort zone, and I write that with a health warning. If you step out of your comfort zone too far you will go straight into the scary zone which can become panic. You do not want to go there if you can avoid it, and you can.

If you step out too far, too soon, too quickly, without planning and preparation you very probably won't enjoy the experience and will immediately return to your comfort zone saying:

- I'm not doing that again.
- It was too hard
- It was too tough
- It was too difficult.
- It was too scary

and of course this all depends on how courageous you are and what fears you have. What one person fears another doesn't; what one person sees as the norm another will see as petrifying.

We are all different even though we can have a tendency to look the same or similar to our peer group.

The ideal way of coming out of your comfort zone is to come out in incremental steps. So try something new. Try something different and do it bit by bit so your comfort zone grows into your growth zone and becomes the new you.

The bigger your comfort zone becomes, the more people you will be able to deal with. The more situations and habits will become the norm. Anything that comes at you will be managed better than you did previously because you have grown and developed.

Your risk zone becomes less as does your scary zone because you are growing and taking on new thoughts and adopting new behaviours.

Even with planning and preparation, stepping out of your comfort zone will raise anxiety and generate a stress response. This is good as it results in an enhanced level of concentration and focus. It keeps you on your toes, literally in some instances as it is the beginning of the flight and flight natural body response to a perceived dangerous situation.

Pressure is good in certain amounts – continued unmanaged pressure turns to stress, which is not good.

Comfort zones can be a nice place to be for a while but not somewhere to stay permanently – if you do not keep up with a fast - changing world you will leave yourself to a torrent of change.

Which can result in a complete feeling of overwhelm where things may end up in the 'too hard' basket or the 'I don't know where to start' basket.

Start small and safely with change, or jump in with both feet. It depends entirely on you, your personality and risk profile. Do something though each action compounded gets you somewhere closer to where you want to be.

If you repeat something often enough and achieve success, however small that may be initially, your confidence will build as repetition creates new habits.

The Unconscious, Preconscious and Conscious Mind

> *"The conscious mind determines the actions, the unconscious mind determines the reactions; and the reactions are just as important as the actions."*
>
> **E. Stanley Jones**

Theories about the unconscious mind vary widely within psychological circles; the truth is that it's hard to prove any of the theories. Just as we know the universe is infinite, we know that the unconscious mind is powerful.

And if you didn't know it was powerful you do now – your unconscious is your protector and driver.

Knowledge of the unconscious mind is limited, but what you cannot do is see it as an enemy power. The unconscious mind cannot become a scapegoat for every failure, mistake or unwarranted reaction that you display.

The unconscious mind is a tool which when managed and treated with respect, can be used to get you to where you want to go. You have to treat it with love and respect as its main purpose is to keep you safe. It has a wisdom of its own.

The Conscious Mind – just the tip of the iceberg

The conscious mind is inside of your current awareness. This is the aspect of your mental processing that you can think and talk about in a rational way. It is the bit that sits between your ears. The conscious mind involves all of the things that you are currently aware of and thinking about. It is somewhat akin to short-term memory and is limited in terms of capacity. Your awareness of yourself and the world around you are part of your consciousness.

People describe themselves as left or right brainers, and we will all tend towards one or the other. The two hemispheres communicate information, such as sensory observations, to each other; they operate both independently and in concert with each other. Each hemisphere performs a fairly distinct set of operations

In general, the left hemisphere is dominant in language: processing what you hear and handling most of the duties of speaking. It's also in charge of carrying out logic and exact mathematical computations. When you need to retrieve a fact, your left brain pulls it from your memory.

The right hemisphere is mainly in charge of spatial abilities, face recognition and processing music. It performs some math, but only rough estimations and comparisons. The brain's right side also helps us to comprehend visual imagery and make sense of what we see. It plays a role in language, particularly in interpreting context and a person's tone.

The conscious mind includes such things as the sensations, perceptions, memories, feeling and fantasies.

The preconscious mind – sits just below the surface

Closely allied with the conscious mind is the preconscious mind, which includes the things that we are not thinking of at the moment but which we can easily draw into conscious awareness.

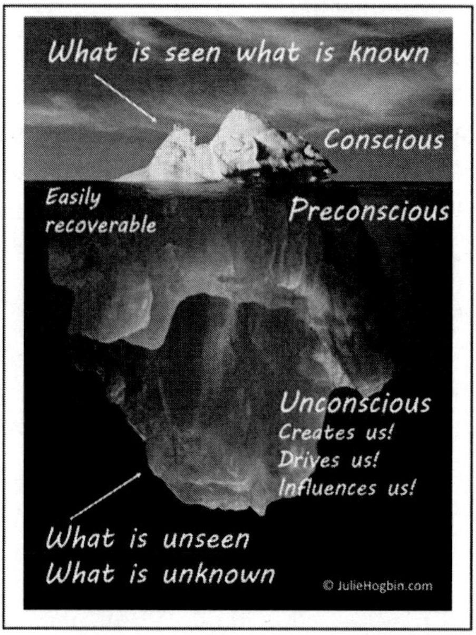

The preconscious mind is a part of the mind that corresponds to ordinary memory. These memories are not conscious, but we can retrieve them to conscious awareness at any time.

While these memories are not part of your immediate awareness, they can be quickly brought into awareness through conscious effort. For example, if you were asked what television show you watched last night or what you had for breakfast this morning, you would be pulling that information out of your preconscious.

The unconscious mind – sits deep and unseen below the surface

Things that the conscious mind wants to keep hidden from awareness are repressed into the unconscious mind. We are unaware of these feelings, thoughts, urges and emotions; Things that are in the unconscious are only available to the conscious mind in disguised form. For example, the contents of the unconscious might spill into awareness in the form of dreams and will appear in our reverse speak, and can also be accessed through certain NLP techniques.

Our unconscious mind:

Preserves the body: One of its main objectives is the survival of your physical body. It will fight anything that appears to be a threat to that survival. So if you want to change something more easily, show, convince and explain to your unconscious how that behaviour is hurting your body and how change will help longer term.

Runs the body: The unconscious handles all of your basic physical functions, such as breathing, heart rate and immune system. Rather than telling the unconscious what perfect health looks like, try asking it what it knows and what you need for better health.

Is like a 7-year old child: Like a young child, the unconscious likes to serve, needs very clear directions, and takes your instructions very literally. So if you say, “This job is a pain in the neck,” your unconscious will figure out a way to make sure that your neck hurts at work! The unconscious is also very “moral” in the way a young child is moral, which means based on the morality taught and accepted by your parents or surroundings. So if you were taught that “sex is nasty,” your unconscious will still respond to that teaching even after your conscious mind has rejected it.

Communicates through emotion and symbols: To get your attention, the unconscious uses emotions. For example, if you suddenly feel afraid, your unconscious has detected, rightly or wrongly, that your survival is at risk.

Stores and organises memories: The unconscious decides where and how your memories are stored. It may hide certain memories, such as traumas, that have strong negative emotions until you are mature enough to process them consciously. When it senses that you are ready, whether you consciously think you are or not, or when you ask it to, it will bring them up so you can deal with them.

Does not process negatives: The unconscious absorbs pictures rather than words. So if you say, "I don't want to procrastinate," the unconscious generates a picture of you procrastinating. Switching that picture from the negative to the positive takes an extra step. Better to tell your unconscious, "Let's get to work!"

If you tell somebody not to do something you are basically telling them to do it! How many times have you seen children do exactly the thing their parent has told them not to? It's not necessarily them being disobedient; it's just that the negative isn't filtered.

What does this mean for goal setting? Write them positively as though you have achieved them and your unconscious will think you have and help you get there.

Makes associations and learns quickly: To protect you, the unconscious stays alert and tries to glean the lessons from each experience. For example, if you had a bad experience in school, your unconscious may choose to lump all of your learning experiences into the "this is not going to be fun" category. It will signal you with sweaty palms and anxiety whenever you attempt something new.

But if you do well in sports, your unconscious will remember that "sports equals success" and you'll feel positive and energised whenever physical activity comes up.

Decisions – The Compound effect

The Path Untrodden
by Robert Frost

Two roads diverged in a yellow wood,
And sorry I could not travel both
And be one traveller, long I stood
And looked down one as far as I could
To where it bent in the undergrowth;

Then took the other, as just as fair,
And having perhaps the better claim
Because it was grassy and wanted wear,
Though as for that the passing there
Had worn them really about the same,

And both that morning equally lay
In leaves no step had trodden black.
Oh, I kept the first for another day!
Yet knowing how way leads on to way
I doubted if I should ever come back.

I shall be telling this with a sigh
Somewhere ages and ages hence:
Two roads diverged in a wood, and I,
I took the one less travelled by,
And that has made all the difference.

Every decision we make consciously or unconsciously has an effect and impact on our goals and future. It can be the smallest of decisions in a split moment, and it takes us down a different path – I regularly read this poem by Robert Frost as a reminder of how the choices we make take us to a different destination.

It is not always about changing who you are and sometimes It may be!

Courage as a characteristic springs to mind.

Courage is the choice and willingness to do against the odds.

Going against the odds will be different for each and every one of us dependent on our upbringing, our education, our level of personal development and experiences.

They could be physical, economical, personal or very simply our peer group.

Courage is about changing what you do. Jeff Olson has written a book, called *The Slight Edge*, which I recommend you read, around the compound effect of the decisions we make.

We make thousands of decisions a day, and each small incremental decision to do something or not ends up, compounded, in the results we have.

The results you have could be exactly the same as you have now, or with change the results that you dream of.

Very, very little in life is a quick win. Most things that are worth having take time, energy and commitment.

- Shifts happen when we stop accepting
- Shifts happen when we stop taking things for granted
- Shifts happen when we stop resting on our 'laurels'
- Shifts happen when we start to look at what we do, question what we do and do something different
- Shifts happen when we challenge ourselves and others
- Shifts happen when we self-analyse and make different choices
- Shifts happen when we keep the momentum going with each little action
- Shifts happen when we recognise our self-sabotage, talk to our inner voice and change how we operate

The slight edge is relentless and cuts both ways: simple disciplines or simple errors in judgement, repeated consistently over time, make or break you.

Simple daily disciplines - small productive actions, repeated consistently over time – add up to the difference between failure and success.

Factor 8 – Carpe Diem

One of my philosophies in life is the Latin phrase 'Carpe Diem' which is usually translated from the Latin as 'seize the day.' Now the purists with Latin may not agree with the translation but I use it as we have one life – let's not waste it, let's live it how we want to live it, let's take control, let's be the person or business we want to be – it is our choice; let's make it happen – get out of bed with a spring in your step and a smile on your face.

There is no time like the present – what are you waiting for? Tomorrow never comes!

Myths of time

- You cannot stop it, save it, bend it or recover it
- It does not fly
- It does not stand still
- It does not go faster when you are enjoying yourself
- You cannot manage it
- Time is money

Time is so much more than money; time is life itself!

Why do some people move mountains and others appear only to move molehills in the same time?

Facts of time

60 seconds in a minute,
60 minutes in an hour,
24 hours in a day,
7 days in a week and
52 weeks in a year

It is finite

- Everything takes time
- We have no control over it

We all have the same it is how you use it that makes the difference – use it wisely in relation to your goals and life.

> *There are seven days in the week and someday isn't one of them!*

> **You physically cannot manage time; all you can manage is the activities you do!**
>
> **Small tweaks can make a big difference - The best approach is to start out with a few small things. Progress in this context might mean that you find yourself with some additional time each day when you can reflect and think. Even if it's just an additional 20 or 30 minutes each day, that's progress.**
>
> **Julie Hogbin**

Procrastination

Procrastination is putting off what you know you need to do, delaying the thing that will move you forward.

Procrastination is the practice of carrying out less urgent tasks in preference to more urgent ones, or doing more pleasurable things in place of less pleasurable ones. Putting off impending tasks to a later time, sometimes to the "last minute" before a deadline and sometimes missing the opportunity completely.

Deadlines do provide a focus that concentrates your mind BUT without the pre-planning the deadline arrives and you haven't started, or haven't left yourself enough time to complete the task at hand.

Everyone procrastinates sometimes, but 20 percent of people chronically avoid difficult tasks and deliberately look for distractions - which, unfortunately, are always available.

Procrastination in large part reflects our perennial struggle with self-control as well as our inability to accurately predict how we'll feel tomorrow, or the next day.

Procrastinators may say they perform better under pressure, but more often than not that's their way of justifying putting things off.

The bright side - It is possible to overcome procrastination; the habit section of this book will help you, writing your plan will help you, and there is a classic very small book to read *Eat that Frog* by Brian Tracy that will help you gain perspective.

Pareto Principle -- The 80/20 Rule

My belief is this is one of the few things that when you get it will revolutionise the way you think and act – it applies itself to all activities in your life.

Work it out and see it come true – look at your everyday life and it will be there – it should be used by every intelligent person on the planet! A great book to read on this subject is *The 80/20 Principle* by Richard Koch.

Pareto's Principle is named after the man who first discovered and described the 80/20 phenomenon, Vilfredo Pareto (1848-1923) who was an Italian economist and sociologist.

He was fascinated by social and political statistics and trends, and the mathematical interpretation of socio-economic systems.

He first observed the 80/20 principle when he was researching and analysing wealth and income distribution trends in nineteenth-century Europe, and he noted that 20 percent of the people owned 80 percent of the wealth!

Pareto then tested his 80/20 principle on all sorts of other distribution scenarios, by which he was able to confirm that the

80/20 principle could be used reliably as a model to predict and measure and manage all kinds of effects and situations.

The reasons why 80/20 has become the norm are:
- The 80/20 correlation was the first to be discovered
- It remains the most striking and commonly occurring ratio
- Since its discovery, the 80/20 ratio has always been used as the name and basic illustration theory

At a simple level the Pareto Principle suggests that where two related data sets or groups exist: inputs and outputs, cause and consequences, effort and results, they will basically fall into the 80/20 arena.

The 80/20 Rule can be applied to anything, from the science of management to the physical world, to the clothes in your wardrobe!

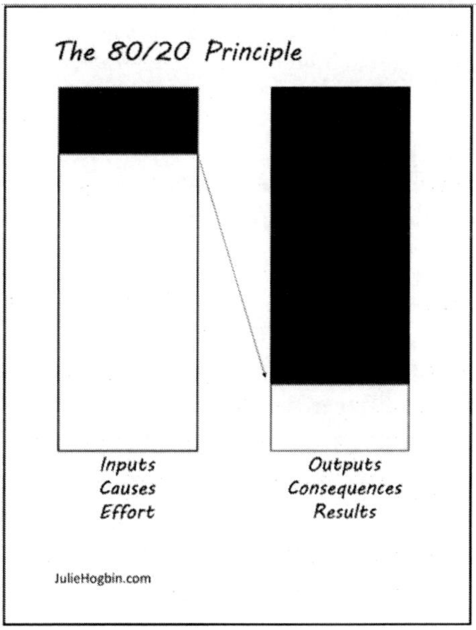

Examples of how it works:
80% of your grief comes from 20% of your associates
80% of results come from 20% of efforts
80% of activity will require 20% of resources
80% of usage is by 20% of users
80% of revenue comes from 20% of customers
80% of problems come from 20% of causes
80% of profit comes from 20% of the product range
80% of complaints come from 20% of customers
80% of sales will come from 20% of sales people
80% of work absence is due to 20% of staff
80% of road traffic accidents are caused by 20% of drivers
80% of a restaurant's turnover comes from 20% of its menu
80% of hits are on 20% of websites
80% of your joy comes from 20% of your activities
80% of your results will come from 20% of the people you know
80% of the difficulty in achieving something lies in 20% of the challenge

The 80/20 rule is not a magic formula; sometimes the relationship between results is closer to 70/30 or 90/10. It is the principle that counts

There are the 'vital few' and the 'trivial many'. The key is defining your vital few, the 20% of your activities that will provide you with the 80% results.

The other trick is avoiding the trivial many, the 80% that will swallow your time and energy and take you down the wrong path. These are the 'things' that you probably do as a quick win; they are the distractions, the things you like doing rather than the ones you know you should be doing.

Identify and focus on the vital few, the 20% they will get you further and quicker than anything else ever will. This is vital when you are aiming to achieve your goals and focus your activities.

This really is a formula to work with in your life – never underestimate it.

Creating a simple timeline

A timeline is a visual picture of what needs to happen and when. It has an end date, a start date and milestones dates between the two.

The purpose of a timeline is to:

- Assess when you need to start a piece of work to achieve the deadline
- Allow you to allocate time to each activity that creates the overall achievement of your goal.
- Allow you to review and evaluate the successful completion of the goal by the fact that you have met each milestone along the way
- Enable you to know that to achieve a certain goal by a certain date that you possibly should have started yesterday!
- Indicate when you need to be more focused with your activities and time
- Allow you to recognise when something in your diary needs to change.
- Tell you what you need to intervene in and it will enable you to predict any issues that may be on the horizon
- Allow you to see the memory joggers in your diary
- Allow you to generate your processes and KPIs if you need to

- Enable you to communicate your plan to others.
- Provide you with a reminder of what you should be doing and when you should be doing anything

And most importantly, it will allow you to evaluate the whole process after the piece of work is completed, so that you can learn for the next time, if and when you do a similar thing.

There are many systems and processes that you can follow. This simple timeline has an end date, start date and points in between that can design to assess your progress. It can be on a piece of paper with post it notes or on a fancy computerised programme – whatever works for you.

You can work forwards to create your own deadline or work backwards from a date set for you – it works both ways.

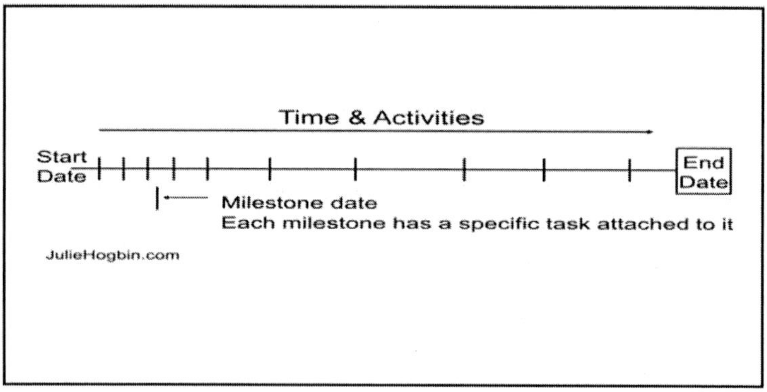

The 5 P's

Pre planning prevents poor performance

A timeline can be done for an hour, a day, a week, months and years depending on the size of the project. It can be complex with multiple layers.

Timelines do work well, and the more you practice the more you will understand them.

> **See it, say it, write it, truly believe it both internally and externally, take action, persevere and it shall be yours**
>
> **Julie Hogbin**

Final words from the author

It is almost as though, when we want to do something differently, we do need a little bit of pixie dust. In reality, though, it's not pixie dust we need; it is the perseverance, dedication, skill set, mindset, knowledge, passion and enthusiasm, just to list a few of the characteristics that we need.

The path to success in any walk of life is never a straight line. As with the plane we are probably off-track 95% of the time, whether that's consciously or unconsciously.

The trick is to be self-aware enough to notice what's going on, and then brave enough to do something about it.

You can achieve whatever it is you want to achieve, when you truly believe that you deserve it and you truly want it. Your self-sabotage is generally due to a deep - rooted belief that you don't deserve it.

If you are not achieving what it is you want to achieve, analyse why. Look at the root cause and do something about it.

This book provides you with a lot of the background information as to what goes on beneath the surface. It also provides you with some solid sound principles and theories of how to practically design the goals for you.

We are not programmed to work alone; we are pack animals. Gain support before it gets too tough and you give up. Write and speak all your goals positively, as though you have already achieved them – use 'towards' language rather than 'away' language and don't use that word you just read! The brain does not compute it so you are telling yourself or someone else to do it rather than to not do it!

As the author of this book, I wish you the very best of luck sprinkled with magic and pixie dust to achieve your life's desires.

The Path to Success

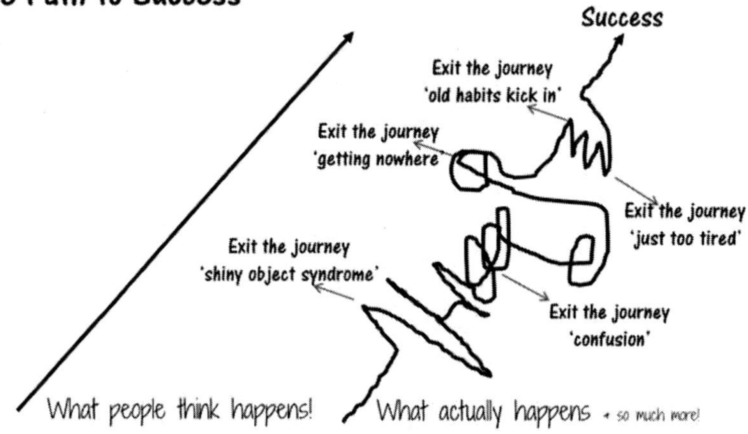

And a final quote from a great man

> **Discipline is the bridge between goals and accomplishment."**
>
> **Jim Rohn**

Good luck with your journey and your change – the more you work at it the luckier you will get!

Final note

If you would like to connect with me please do through one of the above channels or on LinkedIn - I would love to hear your thoughts on this book, my first.

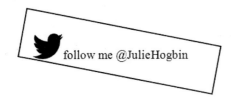

#BusinessTalks
#WealthWiseWomen
#PropertyInvestingExplained

follow me @JulieHogbin

https://www.facebook.com/BusinessTalksandWorkshops/
https://www.facebook.com/WealthWiseWomen/
https://www.facebook.com/SmartPropertyUK/